Bridges not Barriers

BRIDGES
not
BARRIERS

A new rapprochement
in North-South relations

▼ ▼ ▼ ▼

HAMAD BIN ABDULAZIZ AL-KAWARI

Translated by: Basma Elshayyal

Hamad Bin Khalifa University Press
P O Box 5825
Doha, Qatar

www.hbkupress.com

Jsoor la Aswar

First published in Arabic by Hamad Bin Khalifa University Press, 2022.

All rights reserved.

No part of this publication may be reproduced or transmitted in any form or by any means, electronic or mechanical, including photocopying, recording, or any information storage or retrieval system, without prior permission in writing from the publishers.

No responsibility for loss caused to any individual or organization acting on or refraining from action as a result of the material in this publication can be accepted by HBKU Press or the author.

First English edition in 2023

Hamad Bin Khalifa University Press

ISBN: 9789927164897

Printed in Doha-Qatar.

Qatar National Library Cataloging-in-Publication (CIP)

Kawwārī, Ḥamad ʿAbd al-ʿAzīz, author.

[جسور لا أسوار]. English

   Bridges not barriers : a new rapprochement in North-South relations / Hamad Bin Abdulaziz AL-Kawari ; translated by Basma Elshayyal.- First English edition. - Doha, Qatar : Hamad Bin Khalifa University Press, 2023.

   208 pages ; 24 cm

Includes bibliographical references.

Translation of: جسور لا أسوار: مقاربة جديدة لعلاقات الشمال بالجنوب.

ISBN 978-992-716-489-7

   1. Arab countries -- Intellectual life -- 21st century. 2. Arab countries -- Politics and government -- 21st century. 3. Culture conflict. 4. International relations. 5. East and West. 6. Diplomats --Qatar. 7. Unesco -- Elections. I. Elshayyal, Basma, translator.

DS36.88 .K89125 2023
909.0974927– dc 23   202328728592

Contents

Foreword 11

Introduction 13
    A Mercurial Performance 22
    A Persistent Unease. 25

Chapter One. 27
The Son of the Desert – an Unfettered Perspective on
Civilisation 27
    UNESCO – A Potential Beacon, Guiding us Through
        the World's Storms? 32
    The Crux of the Matter 33
    American Peace 36
    The Middle Kingdom 38
    Egypt, a Manipulation in Three Dimensions 40
    Lebanon – the Cracked Mirror 45
    France – a Total Eclipse 47
    French Media Sleepwalks into Disgracing the City of Light. 50
    A Paradox Planted by Hollande along the Champs-Élysées 53
    The Rock in my Life 56
    Falling into a Culture War 57
    A Personal Test – Diametrically Opposed to Accepting
        the Other 63
    Building Bridges, not Barriers 66
    The Tale of the Two Brothers' Wall 68

Chapter Two 73
Striving to Restore the Balance Between East and West 73
    A Deep Chasm. 73

    The Mirage of Diversity 76
    A Continuous Quest. 78
    The Chapter of Grievances 82

Chapter Three. 85
"All the rivers flow into the sea, yet the sea is not full."
Arabs' Contributions to the Arts, Humanities and Literature . 85
    Has Orientalism Really Disappeared?. 85
    Slogans on Progress – Two Sides of the Coin 89
    This – the West – is the Pinnacle of Civilisation! 92
    When Europe Loses her Memory 96
    Arabian Lights 101
    Arab Civilisation and the System of State Governance. 103
    Examples of Arab Muslim Contributions to the Field
        of Science 110
    Arabs' Contributions to the Arts and to the Humanities
        and Literature 115
    Influence and Favour. 126
    From the Past Towards the Future 130

Chapter Four 141
Soft Power 141
    What is not Overcome by Coercion is won Over
        by Gentleness. 141
    The Diplomacy of Gifts 144
    A Holistic Acculturation Process 147
    A Gift's Functions: Enhancing Knowledge
        and Witnessing History. 149
    Harun Al-Rashid and Charlemagne 152
    Arab Soft Power in the Heart of Europe:
        The Arab World Institute 153
    Principles of Cultural Diplomacy. 158
    Selected Means of Cultural Diplomacy 162

Culture and the Rainbow of Diplomacy 166
The Direction of the Compass. 168
On the new global cultural diplomacy 169
Cultural Diplomacy and Sports Wagers. 171

Chapter Five. **177**
The Civilisation
of Cultural Dialogue 177
Dialogue in the Majlis. 180
International Majalis and the Patronage of Senior
Princes and Ministers. 187
Translation is the Mirror of the Islamic Civilisation
and its International Capital 189
And say: "Go forth unto the world.". 195

Conclusion. **201**
Mutual Understanding means accepting the Other 201
A Glut in the North and Famine in the South 205

"Bridges have souls; and the bridges that people cross can never be reliable or safe... they can collapse, they can be swept away by torrents; and they may be infected with diseases like animals."

Foreword

It is difficult – in the civilisational context in which we live – for an intellectual to remain on the fence. The virtue of his presence in society lies in his commitment to issues of humanity as well as his efforts alongside other societal actors in striving to create an awareness of the current challenges that our Arab Islamic civilisation is experiencing during this historic period; one in which international relations between the global North and South are characterised by confusion and crises and demarcated by conflicts and tensions.

Throughout my life, I have worked to meld both theoretical principles and pragmatic practice, for the cerebral thinker is not merely a maker of ideas – rather, he should become meaningfully and practically engaged so that his ideas do not remain imprisoned in abstract realms, incapable of practical implementation; an idea's very essence lies in finding its way towards benefiting people and improving their condition.

Amongst my many experiences was my nomination to the post of UNESCO Director General, where my ideas and aspirations collided with reality. I detail these in my book *The Injustice of Relatives*, in which I shine a spotlight on the injustices that befell me, meted out by my own kith and kin as a result of their contentions, disunity and plotting, with the aim of wasting an opportunity for one of their own who was deserving of office and the responsibilities that it entails.

Likewise, I expose how the West, cloaked in Islamophobia, exploited the disagreements between Arabs and their disparate vote to win with their own unified voice. They continued to impose their perspective onto southern civilisations and obstructed an Arab from leading the organisation by denying the Arab Islamic civilisation's role as a matter of principle, thus strengthening their stranglehold on international organisations. Instead of seizing this opportunity to build bridges, the West continued to erect barriers in this manner.

I refrained from translating *The Injustice of Relatives* into foreign languages in order not to wash our linen in public, preferring instead to write my book *La civilisation opprimée* (The Oppressed Civilisation). This was translated into Spanish and focuses on the role played by the North in persecuting the South and preventing an Arab from taking the helm of the United Nations Educational Scientific and Cultural Organisation. I perceived myself duty-bound to shift the Arabic edition's focus towards the virtues of Arab Islamic civilisation and its favours upon the West, aiming to kill two birds with one stone. Firstly, to remind this generation of Arabs of their own heritage, which has been seemingly forgotten because of their infighting, disunity and wilful disregard of their role in building human civilisation. Secondly, to call for the building of bridges instead of the erection of barriers in the spirit of a renewed rapprochement between the hitherto polarised global North and global South.

Introduction

An image remains, etched in my mind, despite many years having passed since I represented my country at the United Nations in New York. It is an image of my fellow diplomats, fraught with anxiety and with expressions of confusion and helplessness writ large all over their faces as they try their best to reach sometimes seemingly impossible solutions that would end a war or bring about a peaceful settlement between relentlessly fighting forces. It is an image that leads me to state that meaning is extrapolated from the history of human civilisation. I do not deny that this verb is one I glean from my perspective as an Arab, as I cannot divest myself of my heritage and culture without also becoming detached from the cultures of the world or departing from the concept of a "banquet of knowledge", the fruits of which have nourished me over the years.

I was greatly enamoured by Amin Maalouf's literary journey and the way in which he blends both literary and historical approaches, deftly interweaving questions on the civilisational relationship between the Self and the Other amongst pages of his novels. Maalouf's *The Crusades through Arab Eyes* led me to lengthy contemplation, where he addresses the "real narrative" as opposed to the "Othering"; a narrative never posited by Westerners with regard to two centuries of conflict between the Arabs and the "Franks". He draws upon Arab chroniclers' testimonials as primary sources when crafting events and developments within his narrative. This is a narrative that has been neglected for centuries, for we as Arabs understood none other than the narrative woven by the West, received uncritically and imbibed as axiom; whereas

Maalouf's narrative shook these presuppositions to their core whilst offering the neglected perspective on two centuries' worth of war that undoubtedly continue to shape the Arabs' relationship with the West to our present day.

The simple idea envisaged by Amin Maalouf focused on a fresh narrative of the Crusades based on the documented facts, lived experiences and perspectives of contemporaneous Arab historians and chroniclers. This narrative was born into a global historical context in which the world experienced a general apathy and stagnation when it came to Arab relations with the West as well as breakdown of dialogue and growing misunderstanding between both East and West. Within this narrative, my eye was particularly drawn to the distinctly shrewd reference that compels us to revisit the West's relationship with the East – one which alerts us to the fact that Arab historians never spoke of the "Crusades". Instead, they refer to Frankish wars and invasions, which indicates that the use of religion as a façade to these wars did not emanate from the Arab as they did not perceive them to be religious in any case. Rather, it was the West who linguistically clothed this conflict in religious garb, which continues to overshadow relationships between the Western world and Arab world today.

Maalouf never sought to condemn the Other as he had extracted reliable Arab sources for these facts insofar that he strove to achieve a historical impartiality which would restore and reformat relationships between the West and the East, for it is impossible to build a present and a future for generations who are bereft of collective references pertaining to their culture, heritage and civilisation. Before understanding the present, we must understand the past.

Naturally, we are not alone in harbouring reservations about Western discourse. Others hailing from different civilisations have the self-same reservations. Just as the West describes wars between the Arabs and the Franks as Crusades, the West also takes the initiative to label its occupation of the New World with the term "discovery", thus excising the original population's actual existence – an original population who neither perceived the racist expansionist European project as a "discovery", nor considered this "New World" to be new.

Perceptions are disguised within terminology, and language becomes a home for positionality, vis-à-vis the Other. What is truly disturbing is that this language is prevalent and pervasive as a result of civilisational predominance, progressively drawing a veil over nations' consciousness until they surrender to these labels and regard them as facts when they are no more than an articulation of the Western narrative's perspective, which continues to retain supremacist tendencies.

It is this which caused me to observe the fruits of historical misunderstanding between ourselves and the West despite the diversity of my colleagues in the corridors of the UN Security Council, and it is a misunderstanding that encompasses other civilisations and cultures, too. I saw this misunderstanding's foregone conclusion in my colleagues' faltering footsteps, for they would face a hollow emptiness, unable to devise solutions to the successive cycle of problems between nations, even though they were determined to establish peace amongst humanity.

Tragically, they resembled an acrobat walking across a tightrope over a chasm with no safety net to protect them should they fall, nor recourse to any aid that would assist their balance and help preserve their life.

For a long time, I wondered: was this scenario the result of a deterioration in international relations, or the product of decades – perhaps centuries – of inter-civilisational misunderstanding? Is this not due to the "dominant civilisation's" neglect of other civilisations' voices? Does this self-same civilisation, given its current definitions, choose whether to categorise us as civilised or "barbarians"? How can this categorisation possibly contribute to achieving world peace?

I am confident that the status quo is born of concepts that essentially permeate Western thought, despite its cultural discourse and its institutions that call for equality between nations. Successive crises in global dialogue remind me of these chains that shackle subconscious thought behind glittering speeches that elevate international norms yet fail to find a solution to the simplest international disagreement.

I vividly remember Friedrich Engels' analysis of France's occupation of Algeria, celebrating it as an important civilisational development and claiming that this invasion was the ideal method by which the of countries of Tunisia and Libya would also set foot on the path to civilisation. Similarly, his friend Karl Marx defended British Rule in India, claiming that had it not been for British intervention, the social revolution would not have taken place. He granted the British a double mandate: destroying the structures of Asian societies and building the material foundations of a Western society in Asia!

These are ideas that belong to those who fought the capitalist system and criticised Western civilisation, yet their views are shocking in relation to the peoples of Asia and North Africa, as they legitimise occupation under the pretext of social transition. In any case, it is a "Western construct" par excellence, which is to say that neither deviate from the core concept sustaining Western colonialist thought – the claim that Western civilisation is superior to all other civilisations.

Whilst immersed in this retrospection and thinking of this dark situation, I felt a bitter irony as the words of Mahatma Gandhi rang in my ears, answering the question posed to him: "What do you think of Western civilisation?" with "I didn't know they had one!" There is no doubt that Gandhi was a deeply discerning visionary who acknowledged the West's actual possession of civilisation whilst simultaneously doubting the moral dimensions of a society that would lead it colonise nations, abuse peoples and treat them as lacking in humanity.

Likewise, there is no doubt that crises lead to a surge of ideas and push previously concealed ones to the surface. Regardless of whether these crises are economic or political in nature, they inevitably place nations' and organisations' policies and positions squarely on the touchstone of civilisation, revealing its true perception of the Other. The world faced a defining historical moment during the COVID-19 pandemic, exacerbated by the United Nations' impotence in failing to co-ordinate operations in response to unexpected crises which lead to internal instability and ultimately dealt it a deadly blow.

The manner in which the UN faced COVID-19 via the World Health Organisation – one of its own agencies – threw these shortcomings into stark relief. It demonstrated the true extent of its shambling fragility and shameful disunity and exposed the real absence of global consensus and international co-operation that was previously concealed behind closed doors, in addition to the selfish attitudes and narrow interests espoused by specific parties.

Never, since the founding of the United Nations in 1948, has an American president so vulgarly condemned an international organisation concerned with the health of humanity. In fact, Trump's uncouthness plumbed even greater depths when he decided to freeze America's large financial contribution. Perhaps he was inspired by a similar decision taken in 2012 by his predecessor when Washington announced the discontinuation of America's financial contribution to the UN at a time when it was most direly in need.

Thirty years after the end of the Old World Order and the fall of the Berlin Wall, these factors cause us to become increasingly aware that we live in a nebulous world first, in this, the first quarter of the 21st century.

Since the emergence of the New World Order, the world has not enjoyed peace, security or stability. Quite the opposite, the arms race has continued and the spectre of war looms large over more than one place in the world. The gap between rich and poor has widened and nationalist, populist thinking dominates the political landscape in many countries all over the world. Western literature has begun to warn of "the death of democracy", "the demise of liberalism" and the regression of multilateral policies in favour of unilateral ones.

The hopes and dreams of those who advocate for peace were dissipated by this bleak picture, and further dampened by the erosion of the United Nations' original maxims and the lacklustre performance of its member organisations including that responsible for culture, UNESCO.[1] The process of evaluating and reviewing these infrastructures has become an absolute necessity in this current time in response to demands of intellectuals, organisations and various countries that have, for years, called upon the United Nations to begin a period of reform. This is in addition to the special conference dedicated to "revitalising discourse on United Nations reforms" that was hosted in Qatar's capital city, Doha, as part of a general overhaul of reforms to the UN.

It becomes manifestly clear to us that the initial aims, present in 1945 and determined by the founding fathers, have become unattainable. It is this that makes me utterly convinced that the world "post COVID-19" will not be as promising as we imagine unless those who are sincerely determined and resolute act. This was unequivocally heralded by dangers lurking in our societies in

---

[1] See: Al-Kawari: Hamad bin AbdulAziz "It's Time to Reform the UN" 12th May 2020. Published in seven languages on the Project-syndicate website https://www.project-syndicate.org/commentary/united-nations-covid19-response-shows-need-for-reform-by-hamad-bin-abdulaziz-al-kawari-2020-05?barrier=accesspaylog

the first quarter of the 21ˢᵗ century, once again putting all the UN maxims to the test.

Undoubtedly, today, we live in the midst of unprecedented, accelerated change – change that forces the world to confront unexpected challenges. Humanity has experienced many catastrophes throughout its long history and incurred major losses due to natural disasters, or human suffering as a result of wars and conflicts, but it has never witnessed anything similar to the novel coronavirus. It was anticipated that the UN as an organisation would galvanise humanity's capability when confronting the dangers of COVID-19, but the hopes that people pinned on this organisation vanished like castles in the air. With great regret, what we are witnessing today is the collapse of a world and the beginning of the birth of another, unknown world - the delivery of which the UN has failed to play a central role. The greater problem is that we are, once again, watching the rise of right-wing currents hostile to the Other and civilisation being torn apart afresh.

During the pandemic, terror gripped everyone for many months and overshadowed all other considerations. It seems to me that the population of the entire globe was shocked, caught short on the brink of this abyss that appeared before their eyes as they observed mandatory quarantine in their homes, precipitately cut off from the outside world. Suddenly, quite literally overnight, everyone realised our vulnerability to exceptional dangers in every sense of the word. After almost everyone had ignored previous warnings, considering them to be routine in much the same way fire, flood and other natural warnings are, they now realised that this was on a different scale, and that death would reap souls in their thousands with an invisible scythe.

Our short-term memory helps us recall images of catastrophes that have befallen humanity in recent years and which we relive through nightmares rather than dreams. People were suddenly confronted by the SARS (severe acute respiratory syndrome) epidemic in 2003. Panic and terror spread amongst them after they thought it was merely seasonal flu. This was followed by the 2008 mortgage crisis, which brought to mind the global economic crisis of 1929 that would have laid everything to waste, had it not been for the involvement of nations who bailed out the most prominent banks, saving them from liquidation.

Following this, the world was suddenly exposed to the roars of Eyjafjallajökull – the Icelandic volcano– and its vast plumes of volcanic ash that rose as high as nine kilometres into the sky, creating a black cloud that crippled air travel around the world and caused an unprecedented environmental disaster across Northern Europe.

During these painful, successive disasters, the American Bill Gates demonstrated characteristic sobriety and intuition by announcing in 2017: "When I was young, the threat of a nuclear war terrified us. Now I think that what will kill 10 million people over the next decades will surely be an infectious virus and not a war". And now Bill Gates' prediction has come true; and a pandemic has taken over the world, shaking humans' tranquillity, just as it has destroyed many maxims that have reverberated for years in the halls and on the podia of the UN, and still it remains incapable of responding to the challenges of this era. However, this fraught and nebulous situation motivates those with an active conscience to shoulder the historical responsibility of correcting the trajectory of international organisations that were established in order to serve people and advocate for their rights, wherever they may be. Given this historical context, I cannot but remain committed to maintaining lofty ideals and moral principles as the primary reference point for all dealings and practices within the UN. It is a commitment that I have never deviated from in the slightest throughout my work in various capacities, held over four decades in various international organisations, but particularly in the United Nations.

There is no doubt that my posts in the UN have granted me the opportunity to strive for rapprochement between the North and

South; and to work towards achieving tangible results separate to hollow political protocol that leaves one empty-handed. However, my commitment to this struggle never once prevented me from being critical of this bureaucratic behemoth whilst acknowledging the role this international organisation has played in embedding security by ending international conflict, protecting human rights and ending the occupation of many countries since the end of the Second World War.

The fact remains that this organisation – an erstwhile, formidable umpire that would pronounce on international conflicts by virtue of its own legal and moral terms of reference – has become in many cases no more than a plaything in the hands of a small yet powerfully influential self-serving coterie who rarely look to the global common good. By doing so, they deny international law, peace, global security and all the other principles for which the UN was established to uphold along with its constituent organisations in the wake of World War Two. Nonetheless, we must, in good faith, gladly acknowledge various successes such as the 1989 "Summit of Storms", which took place in Helsinki between US President George Bush, Sr. and the leader of the former Soviet Union, Mikhail Gorbachev, where the UN nurtured a meeting which resulted in an agreement that opened Russia up to an era of democracy, even though it has not lasted till our present day. Despite this, the summit heralded the end of the Cold War, thus ending an era of bipolar global power dynamics and beginning an era in which the United States of America assumed unilateral hegemony.

No sane person would doubt that the UN has ceased to be the source of succour and supporter of peace that its founders envisaged in the way that it functioned between 1950 and 1970, putting an end to colonisation in particular. Nevertheless, its current state does not permit us – in the words of Trotsky – to consign it (and its most significant member organisations such as UNESCO and the WHO) to "the dustbin of history". This is despite the absence of equality and the arrogance of some larger nations which embolden it against abiding by various international treaties and respecting others. The world witnessed this during the 2017 elections for the post of Director-General in succession to the former Bulgarian Director-General; and the host nation's attack on the Arab candidate who represented the only geographical region that has never held the post. Arab civilisation paid the price for this arrogance and injustice once again when it had hoped to extricate itself from the difficult position of an oppressed and downtrodden society. It had seemed that the bloc of Northern nations would respect the peoples who had historically contributed to the creation of this wonderful civilisation. But it was not to be.

A Mercurial Performance

"Twenty-nine votes for Ms Audrey Azoulay, twenty-nine votes for Mr Hamad Al Kawari." Thus were the results of the election for the position of UNESCO Director-General announced from the podium on Friday October 13th, 2017, by Michael Forbes, German President of the Executive Bureau, the body that brings together the 58 nations who are eligible to vote according to UN regulations. An equal tie was expected, even though the international media and observers had predicted that the Qatari candidate would win.

In this defining moment, everyone believed that the curtain had fallen on an entire act of the electoral battle and that the bell signalling the next round – the tie-breaker – would ring in order that the winner may be determined. Voices subsided and were gradually muffled in the hall into which Michael Forbes' words were hurriedly tossed. Breaths were caught; when I heard the microphone crackle again and everyone turned towards a voice that seemed troubled and hoarse… Suddenly, a heavy silence settled amongst those present. The President's voice resounded once again to announce that a mistake had been made in tallying the votes; and that upon verification it appeared that the result was 30 votes for Azoulay as opposed to 28 for Al Kawari. At this, celebratory shouts from the French candidate's supporters drowned out the uproar that was scattered throughout the hall, drawing everyone's attention, for nobody thought to question the President over what had just taken place and so this mystery remains hidden in those muted, swirling whispers to this day. As the chapters of this story continue to unfold, it is strange to note that the results of the final vote which led to the French candidate becoming UNESCO Director-General are markedly absent from its own website; whereas it has become customary for both proceedings and results to be displayed since 2017.

On this basis, observers still question the credibility of these polls, capricious as they were and entirely devoid of professionalism. The entire world witnessed this as though it were a performance from the Theatre of the Absurd. How can we justify this farcical performance and the election officer's lapses, when he is one of the most prominent officials on the international arena? At this point, I personally became convinced that the intention of this entire shoddy performance was to eliminate competition rather than to face it honourably, despite the campaign's promising start in 2016 – a campaign journey replete with unexpected events!

In writing this book, my intention is not to settle scores; rather the honourable task of faithfully documenting and revealing events as they happened to readers who seek the truth. Above all this, my personal experience stands witness and offers historical testament complete with evidence of a methodological, tendentious campaign that bore no goodwill to the nations of the South. This campaign spared no effort in impeding a fresh start for the UNESCO at the hands of an Arab Director-General who was determined to reform a decrepit international organisation and to breathe new life into its corridors and had made a pledge to his supporters that he would work to restore balance in favour of the nations of the South as well as establish trust and credibility between this prestigious organisation's diverse cultural and social elements.

This opportunity was frittered away as a cloud of mistrust and paranoia loomed over both cultures – Northern and Southern – and the spectre of inter-civilisational conflict reared its ugly head, terrifying the nations of the South afresh. To all those who believed in UNESCO's founding principles, it seemed that these were about to collapse and crumble, just as they were now convinced that the dominant power dynamic and prevalent narrative discourse was entirely Western-centric, favouring the North.

What grieves me is the demise of UNESCO's symbolic value that the world is currently experiencing. What was once a bastion is now merely a lifeless archaeological relic where nothing remains but the images of its founding fathers who had crafted principles for a meritorious human life. I am anxious for the destiny of this institution should active consciences not move to correct its course. Just as I believe deeply in the seminal role that UNESCO has to play in the history of humanity, I am equally acutely conscious of what threatens the world when humanity loses faith in organisations that have pledged to protect societies from hate, conflict and discrimination.

Accordingly, the UN's slogans ring hollow, for what of "…to save succeeding generations from the scourge of war, which twice in our lifetime has brought untold sorrow to mankind"? Does not United Nations' literature proclaim that no race, system or culture is superior to another and that "there is no place for cultural superiority"?

Once again, Arab civilisation faces the "clash of civilisations" just as other civilisations do. The world drowns in fresh failures. Rather than leading us to aimless action, this state of affairs drives us to strive, with unrelenting determination, to correct a global cultural narrative over which the West presides in order that human civilisation may be the provenance of all instead of a blinkered, inwardly looking world view that is only capable of seeing its own steps as time progresses.

A Persistent Unease

What is the way to dispel the disquietude that one feels when the official presiding over the voting process announces an equal tie of 29 votes each to both the Qatari and French candidates, only to state moments later, that the opposing candidate actually received thirty votes instead? Of course, this was no mere slip of the tongue, but sleight of hand executed by the West before the President of the Executive Bureau hurried to collect the ballot papers and lay the files to rest, as the world watched in astonishment with sardonic smiles and bilious throats. It is ironic that he is of Germanic descent, a culture that prides itself on meticulousness and rigour. Here, I would like to share an anecdote. In her commencement speech addressing the graduates of Harvard University entitled "Tear down the walls of ignorance and narrow-mindedness", the German chancellor Angela Merkel began by recalling her simple origins in East Germany before imparting advice which many consider to be her sincerest moral legacy, saying: "We need to be sincere with others and more importantly, to be sincere with ourselves. This means not calling lies truth, nor truth, lies".[1]

The incident involving the recount and the announcement of results was a disturbing one which exposed the Northern nations' true nature and caused its perpetrators to refrain from publicising the results of the votes on the UN website out of sheer embarrassment, despite the publication of all four previous rounds. It constituted the final link in a chain of shameful wheeling and dealing stretching out over two years, overseen by the countries of the North and

---

1 See the US News page in Arabic online, accessed 14/6/2020

aided and abetted by nations who betrayed their own people and intellectuals before betraying their Arab identity. Public statements appeared courteous and dignified when compared with hidden vile, shadowy whispers; aptly embodying wisdoms attributed to the Abbasid poet, Salih bin Abdul Quddus:

> *"No goodness is there in the love of a silver-tongued sycophant, whose words are sweet and whose heart is aflame [with hatred].*
> *He meets you with oaths of trust and fealty, then turns away as a scorpion.*
> *To you, his tongue drips sweet honey – he slinks behind your back, fox-like, into his den."*

History will bear witness that the international stage observed a suppressed consensus on the need to nominate an Arab Director-General; and that the French opponent had no standing in French public opinion yet rode to victory on the coat-tails of considerable support that was voluntarily offered by Arab brothers out of sheer spite, envy and hatred. It is not surprising that she would seek this opportunity to ingratiate herself, to divide and conquer whilst others were squabbling in the edifice of lofty ideals, emerging with an insipid victory reeking of betrayal and intrigue.

Chapter One
The Son of the Desert – an Unfettered Perspective on Civilisation

I am, truly, a son of the desert. For whenever my memory draws me back to my childhood and youth, I feel a genuine, deep-seated sense of belonging to this welcoming vastness where I can sense unlimited freedom flowing through my veins as the sandy winds swirl around me in the Arabian desert. Uncharted winds from unknown directions that lovingly embrace the sand dunes, crafting them into glorious, harmonious forms unmatched by the world's greatest artists. These dunes that stretch out endlessly until they blend into warm waves of the sea at Khawr Al Udayd, a beautiful, sandy, inland gulf in the Southeast of Qatar not far from the neighbouring Kingdom of Saudi Arabia. There, the burning sun rises during the day, to be replaced by an impeccable, unparalleled domed sky through which the light of the stars glitters by night. This glorious beauty manifests itself as mentioned in the Noble Qur'an: "Verily! We have adorned the near heavens with [beautifying] stars" (Al Safat, 37:6).

I love the desert and the sea equally, for both transcend the limits of human vision. Within them, one's gaze and thoughts may be unleashed, free to rove and contemplate deeply. This is a habit that has grown with me since my childhood and remains with me till today, when I choose to sit facing the sea on the beach at home in

Burj Laffan, North Qatar. Throughout my childhood, I never knew barriers in the form of walls. And I never imagined the existence of these repulsive barriers, erected here and there throughout the ages to separate humans from each other. They violate vision, and their architects remain ignorant that they are, in fact, building high the walls of their own jail before erecting a prison for others.

One of the strange paradoxes of our world is that the expansion of urbanisation – and hence boundaries – throughout the globe was accompanied by a digital revolution which removed borders. However, many insist on denying the Other, treating them with contempt and distancing them from decision-making circles or any other of human dignity. It is as though the process of creating and drawing boundaries is set to continue for as long as the colonialist mentality – which people had believed to be waning - does.

Many have forgotten that civilisations were not born overnight, for when a particular cultural narrative gives rise to inflated feelings of superiority, people become short-sighted. Today's civilisation cannot overshadow everyone's perceptions and understanding. How many times has the phrase "belonging to the human civilisation" masked the truth behind various civilisations and their legacies – as if "human civilisations" were the West only, proceeding to command and to be obeyed.

Despite our communal presence and shared existence in this challenging historical era, it is impossible to ignore the fact that human history encompasses far more than this digital age – it is multiple civilisations stretching as far back as the ancient Sumerians and ancient Egyptians, passing through the Aztecs and Incas of Latin America and the Chinese and Indic right up to the Abrahamic civilisations of the present day.

The world cannot deny that the study of the birth, rise and demise of civilisations did not emanate entirely from Western scholarship, nor is it solely their possession. This discipline is not limited to Western historians and anthropologists, for nobody can fail to acknowledge the erudite scholar Ibn Khaldun's seminal role in this field. Max Weber, Arnold Toynbee and Christopher Dawson all offered brilliant analyses on the rise and fall of nations, yet our appreciation of their works should never allow us to forget the pioneering trajectory first mapped out by Ibn Khaldun, an Arab and a Muslim.

I highlight Ibn Khaldun's heritage so that we may become more convinced of the importance of viewing "human civilisation" as an expansive receptacle for cultures and heritages in all their diversity, not a replacement for them. To speak of civilisation in the singular should not detract from the reality that history is built on pluralism. Despite the obsession to profile and pigeonhole everything from ideas to morals in our current era, we remain descendants of diverse civilisations. That is why I stress that I am a son of the desert, professing my allegiance to Arab and Islamic civilisation in all its manifestations and all that entails.

To speak of a "human civilisation" might be helpful when discussing our shared commonalities, but it should not distract us from examining our unique features nor blind us from recognising our areas of diversity which are, after all, the very essence of creation and a vital condition enabling our acquaintance. Talk of a "global civilisation" is petrifying, as it crushes the very pulse of pluralistic civilisations, squanders their symbolic wealth and overlooks their potential. We should be aware that the journey of life is similar to the life of civilisations, for it, too, is built on the discovery of our shared heritage. The length of a civilisation's existence is directly proportional to its interaction with other nations, regardless of how ancient or modern it is. When cultures meet, they cross fertilise, ebb and flow. They draw closer to produce similarities and overlapping identities and diverge based on differences. When one civilisation recedes, another develops. A civilisation might become extinct after a long existence; scattering legends and epics in their wake that cannot be recalled without leaving a lasting mark. The lifespan of these civilisations cannot be measured as we do states or dynasties or ruling systems; for civilisations live longer, flow deeper and have a far greater reach than any ideology. Political systems are fleeting when compared with civilisations. From development to annihilation, civilisations have passed through many systems in the history of humanity, the causes of which have been analysed extensively by historians and sociologists, many of whom differ – yet all agree that growth takes place amid conditions of conflict and challenge.

We are indebted to the British scholar, Edward Burnett Tylor (1832-1917) for his pioneering definition of the concept of culture. Placing it in the wider ethnographic sense, he considered the terms "culture" and "civilisation" to be multifaceted ones that include knowledge, beliefs, art, morals, manners, law and all the other skills and habits acquired by humans as members of society.[1] His definition remains significant, despite the plethora of definitions that followed it over more than a century. Tylor's expansive attitude meant that his concept and definition of human culture was not subject to ethnocentric compartmentalisation or profiling, nor was it satisfied with placing "primitive" cultures in a separate category because he considered all humans to be inherently equal in terms of origin, disagreeing with [contemporaneous] theologians who considered them to be a lesser race.

Whenever we revisit this simple definition, we realise that the intellectual legacy of the West is not entirely subservient to the desires of certain schools of thought or some scholars who rush to brand civilisations and cultures as inherently inferior, helpless and incapable of progress.

Some labour under the delusion that culture is something pure, transcendental and the exclusive property of certain peoples only;

---

1 Edward Burnett Tylor, Primitive Culture: Researches into the Development of Mythology, Philosophy, Religion, Art and Custom, 2 vols. (London: J. Murray, 1871), p.1.

deliberately forgetting that over the centuries, every culture absorbs and assimilates external influences. Just as it is affected by these, it also impacts the surrounding world as its dynamic, fluid existence flows from birth to decline and through to renaissance. At this point, we can now speak of an iterative cultural framework by virtue of dialogue and symbolic transactions between nations, both of which are necessary for human interaction. This condition presupposes that these peoples accept the self-same concept of interaction and that nations pro-actively wish to open their doors to the outside world rather than erect barriers. As the French writer, Antoine de Saint-Exupéry decried: "Humans erect too many walls and do not extend enough bridges." Since ancient times, humans have been obsessed with building barriers, a phenomenon borne out of fear of the Other and the pursuit of self-preservation, considering them to be an enemy and a constant threat. Thus, the Great Wall of China was erected at the start of the second century BC to keep out migrating foreign peoples and to protect the empire from the invasions of nomadic tribes, primarily from Mongolia. In England, Hadrian's wall was built early in the second century at the behest of Hadrian, the Roman emperor, with the intention of preventing incursions by the Picts of modern-day Scotland. The construction of walls and barriers did not come to a halt during ancient or even medieval times but has continued to our present era. Examples include the Berlin Wall, the Israeli apartheid wall, the Kenyan wall along the Somali border and Trump's wall, which he started building under the pretext of preventing uncontrolled migration across the southern border from Mexico.

It is strange that humans are not satisfied with the mountains, rivers and seas that separate nations from one another, but rather began to draw inspiration from each other's experiments in erecting walls, raising fences and digging isolating tunnels that fly in the face of history, geography and nature itself, claiming to safeguard homelands and protect nations from the "enemy without".

UNESCO – A Potential Beacon, Guiding us Through the World's Storms?

Every so often, the annals of history celebrate great men who serve humanity; including intellectuals who, following the devastation of World War II, were bold enough to launch the first clause of UNESCO's founding constitution: "Since wars begin in the minds of men, it is in the minds of men that the defences of peace must be constructed." Seventy years later – after my own experiences in the corridors of UNESCO – I can add: "… and the bridges of dialogue extended to discuss the future of humanity." It is a wish suffused with utopia, for time has taught me the truth of these lines penned by Ahmad Shawqi, Prince of Poets:

> *"Desires can never be achieved by day-dreaming, affairs of the world must be secured by force."*

Ideas that were considered by others to be castles in the air were, to me, a moral duty both towards myself and others. I have embedded the principle of striving for peace deep into my innermost being and made the UNESCO declaration one of the key missions in my life. Yes, I have worked as a diplomat for decades and struggled in the corridors of the Security Council to bring about reconciliation between nations. As an ambassador to my country in several capitals around the world and as a representative to the United Nations and to UNESCO, I have striven hard to secure mutual understanding, dialogue and mutual beneficial exchange. In fact, I followed the same path when I took on the mantle of responsibility at Qatar's Ministry of Culture, Arts and Heritage. That is why the events commemorating Doha as the Capital of Arab Culture, 2010 were characterised by their openness towards all the world's cultures, their acceptance of differences, warm welcome towards others and the building of bridges between visiting intellectuals of every persuasion who hailed from every possible walk of life.

I did not stay away from the political arena for long, returning when I was tasked by my country in 2016 to run as a nominee for the post of UNESCO Director-General – a task that no other Arab succeeded in accomplishing since 1946, for various reasons. I knew that the Northern nations would not welcome an Arab as head of UNESCO, and that they would resort to using all the legitimate and illegitimate means at their disposal in order to prevent a nominee from the South from entering into the arena, the sole preserve of the Northern nations for decades. Even though the UN professes to represent all the world's cultures, racist, supremacist mindsets prevail and colonial legacies run deep in its veins, despite the attempts of the nations of the North to appear otherwise. Nonetheless, I - like thousands of other Arab intellectuals and intellectuals from developing nations – was under the illusion that the UN accommodated everyone, judging by merit alone and not distinguishing between East and West. I believed that we had the right to dream of leading the organisation for the good of humanity without fear or favour. Alas, the organisation's betrayal of its own principles stood solidly in the way of this legitimate dream, thwarting the world's sincere intentions in their entirety.

The Crux of the Matter

The 27th of April 2017 was a decisive day, as is widely known by all. The nominee for the post of UNESCO Director-General must deliver their speech succinctly in less than ten minutes before the 58 members of the UNESCO Executive, then answer their questions and respond to their comments. On that day, the nominee must make full use of the time allocated to him and present an accurate summary of his manifesto, outlining his vision and making it crystal clear without causing the ambassadors of the member nations to become bored. I was destined to be the last speaker as a result of the draw. The seven other nominees preceded me, along with all the advantages and disadvantages that this entailed. One the one hand, I listened to my adversaries' speeches and became familiar with the nature of questions that they were being asked as well as their answers. This, undoubtedly, led me to enjoy the atmosphere of discussion. On the other hand, however, my competitors covered most of the issues that I had identified in my own electoral speech and dealt with in my manifesto, issues that I had analysed and offered recommendations regarding.

Prior to this, I had published several works in different languages with international public opinion in mind and aimed at accredited ambassadors to UNESCO. In these I explained my manifesto and plan to breathe new life into UNESCO, which would represent a beginning of a reform process for the organisation, which was experiencing a deep financial and political crisis. I thought that by assuming the presidency, an Arab who enjoyed the support of wealthy nations and wholeheartedly believes in UNESCO's universal educational, scientific and cultural principles would surely constitute a guarantee to save the institution and fulfil the outlined aims. I thought, and sincerely believed, that in addition to demonstrating transparent procedure, with an executive that operated with no discrimination regardless of a nominee's ethnic or geographic backgrounds, this would preserve equilibrium and equal opportunities for all. I also believed that this speech would convince the accredited ambassadors to UNESCO of the existence of a manifesto worthy of endorsement and support. And this is, indeed, what took place during the discussion.

According to studies and analyses that I had carried out during my campaign and based on my previous experiences in international organisations, I knew that African, South American and Caribbean nations were amongst those who relied more than others on UNESCO to help them advance education, science and culture in their regions, given their urgent need for support, as their conditions differ from those of Europe, the Gulf nations and the Arab Maghreb. To me, Africa was part of the axis of the South that suffered the injustices of the North just as the nations of the Caribbean and South America did.

I was acutely conscious that commitment to this axis was part and parcel of my commitment to human values, for these countries' role in the story of human civilisation cannot be erased. I would tell myself that mighty trees grow from small acorns, and in order to keep this tree of civilisation evergreen, the soil of cultures and values amongst all nations must be fortified.

I began my campaign full of faith in the value of the Southern nations. There was an unspoken agreement across the board internationally indicating that most countries were in favour of an Arab candidate, given that the Arab bloc had never assumed leadership of UNESCO since its inception. This subsequently explains the fury on the Arab streets, public opinion and anger of the overwhelming majority of free-thinking, educated people when a French candidate - Audrey Azoulay - was nominated at the last minute without prior warning.

Four candidates had come forward; myself and one each from Iraq, Lebanon and Egypt. Regret and disquiet still rankle in the Arab world as a result of the events that took place during the two previous rounds when competition between Arab nations intensified to the extent that the Saudi and then the Moroccan candidates were both ruled out. The Egyptian position was shameful, as their entire diplomatic machine was activated in order to secure the Qatari candidate's failure and to support their opponent. History will bear witness that certain Arab countries tried their utmost to ensure that the 11th Director-General of the UNESCO would not be an Arab.

How can any sane person accept such a reckless, irresponsible position from a nation that carries the beacon inherited from the ancient Pharaonic and Islamic civilisations? Moreover, students from all corners of the Arab world generally, and from the Levant in particular, have always found a warm welcome in her capital and in her universities, the doors of which have been open to them over the centuries. It seemed to me that the current Egyptian political narrative no longer recognised the culture that it had inherited, the bricks of which were laid by Egyptian thinkers such as Taha Hussein, Abbas Al Akkad, Zaki Naguib Mahmoud and others of their calibre. How can I forget a single day I spent amongst them as one of their number who came to Cairo to gather knowledge, science and literature – for it was then a Mecca and a shrine for every seeker of knowledge? I became even more sorrowful considering the widening chasm between those at the cutting edge of society, the hopes and dreams of intellectuals, and those responsible for serving culture in Egypt today.

In the face of policies where desires trump conscience, a noble and enlightened cause was stolen from the Arabs. Its goal was to serve Arab civilisation and the civilisations of afflicted nations in the South in the field of international cultural diplomacy. The gulf separating several Arab countries as well as that dividing the nations of the North and the South became apparent through cracks in the imperfect veneer that was erected to conceal them. In light of these hidden conflicts growing in the shadows, I realised the scale and extent of the catastrophe threatening the international community for the first time.

American Peace

The next day, curiosity overcame me. I was keen to find out the international media's reaction to the candidates' contributions to the UNESCO Executive Board members and what they thought of their manifesto presentations, now that they had all been delivered and comparison was possible. The first surprise came by way of the Israeli Press' commentary, presenting professional and impartial reporting – even unequivocally acknowledging the Qatari candidate's clarity of vision and the superiority of his bid. Most observers familiar with UNESCO's inner workings testified that my speech was trustworthy and sound, adding that ambassadors exceeded the time allocated for them to question me because the proposed manifesto sounded so convincing, hence their determination to vote for me.

An amusing anecdote that took place was when the US ambassador who was listening to me speak sought permission from her government to intervene with the intention of embarrassing me. She had, in fact, already taken the floor to ask me: "What will you do to ensure that UNESCO does not become a stage for political tussles?" My extensive experience in working for international organisations stood me in good stead here, so I answered calmly: "The issue is very simple. Absolutely, UNESCO is concerned with education, culture and the sciences; but who can imagine that it is not simultaneously involved in political issues?" Then I decided to give as good as I got and added: "If we follow accepted protocol and choose to speak in false politically correct niceties, we will naturally agree that there is no place for politics in this matter. However, if we lean a little towards truth and speak frankly, then we both know full well that politics is ever-present in all our work. You, for example, are the largest and richest country in the world. Despite this, the United States does not pay its dues to UNESCO as you know. In reality, the cost of a single one of your space rockets would solve UNESCO's financial difficulties in their entirety. That is why your decision to refrain from fulfilling your dues to the UNESCO is, ultimately, a political decision par excellence." I decided, in this moment of blazing honesty, to conclude by calling a spade a spade, saying: "But if you are obliquely referring to the Palestinian-Israeli question should an Arab head UNESCO, I fully understand your concerns regarding impartiality or lack thereof during discussions. I feel it is important to remind you that I previously chaired the

Fourth Committee – responsible for political issues in the United Nations; and I was a neutral arbiter between Palestine and Israel, as required by United Nations laws and regulations. As recently as a few months ago, I was the President of the United Nations Conference on Trade and Development (UNCTAD) from 2012 till 2016, where I adhered to the principles of impartiality as dictated by the nature of this position." It appeared that my answer cut to the quick, because the US representative did not respond – their silence spoke volumes.

The Middle Kingdom

My election campaign included a visit to China, where I was determined to go in order to introduce my manifesto and campaign programme. China, as is known, has been a member of UNESCO since 1946. During this visit, I came to appreciate the significance of the experience that I had gained from my previous post in the United Nations. That a seasoned, veteran Chinese diplomat would meet me in Beijing seemed normal to me. That he was attempting to discover my intentions was far closer to the truth, for I was used to Chinese pragmatism and their consummate skill in homing in on their fellow conversationalists' secrets. I smiled because I had nothing to hide and made it clear that I was canvassing for votes that were needed for the post of UNESCO Director-General. The trick is to refrain from tricks.

Evidently, my frankness had a major impact on my Chinese counterpart as one evening he pro-actively offered me a valuable piece of advice, saying: "I see that you are travelling the world in order to present your programme, and this is admirable. But as the time to cast votes draws near, remember to stay in Paris for a few months in the run up to the elections so that you can meet UNESCO ambassadors daily. They are the ones who will vote, and decisions lie in their hands. Those are the people you should keep close company with, understand their mentality and their real concerns away from formal conventions."

China remains, in my opinion, a world in and of itself. With the greatness of its civilisation, it does not share the principle of equality between nations upon which UNESCO was founded, where the great powers are on an equal footing with the smallest Caribbean nation – one nation, one vote. For thousands of years, China has perceived itself to be a central civilisation – the sun around which other 'lesser' nations orbit, whose remits are restricted to sending ambassadors to the Chinese Imperial Court to pay tribute, surrender their tithes and glean what light they may from the Glorious Middle Kingdom. Despite this self-perception, wherever I went in China, I felt the openness and tolerance of the Chinese; and remembered the Chinese proverb that says: "Verily, a hundred rivers can only flow into the sea because of its huge capacity." Throughout the long course of history, the Chinese people, with all their ethnic variations, have succeeded in creating vibrant civilisations, rich in their glorious diversity.

Whilst China's star faded over the period of 150 years during Western colonialism, it is in the process of regaining its traditional position as a great power. Today, the Middle East and Gulf regions have fast become strategically important from a Chinese perspective, following their use by colonial powers as strategic stepping stones en route to India or China. That is why it strives to expand beyond its direct regional peripheries in order to reflect its traditional, rightful place "under the dome of the sky" or "tianxia" according to Chinese nomenclature. This explains President Xi Jinping's statement: "China must take a central position on the international stage and make a greater contribution to humanity." It is in this context that China's mega project "The Belt and Road Initiative", known simply as "The New Silk Road" should be understood. If all roads led to Rome in ancient times, it is most likely that all roads will lead to China during the 21st century.

What increased my admiration for the Chinese paradigm was the extent to which they are able to contribute meaningfully in the building of the next stage of our human civilisation, for they believe that no two leaves in the world are 100% identical; and each country or nation state is obliged to know its identity, be cognisant of its origins and conscious of where it has come from and where it is headed towards. They attach great importance to strengthening lines of communication with the rest of the world's countries, led by a simple motto: "When thinking about your own interest, you should consider the interests of the many."

Egypt, a Manipulation in Three Dimensions

Anyone who has lived in the desert or in Arab countries generally knows that the autumn season is heralded by the sight of bunches of ripening fruit hanging from the palm trees, as the honeyed sweetness of dates glisten in different colours from pale yellow to deep, rich brown. The bunches of dates crowd together at a height of 10 metres or more, so that mischievous hands cannot get at them. Before humans climb up to harvest them, they may only be reached by swarms of bees who sip from their sealed nectar in order to produce rare and precious date honey. However, these ripe fruits also occasionally attract rowdy children who dare not climb the dangerous tree trunks so satisfy themselves with pelting the bunches with stones so that some of the dates drop to the ground. The children then devour these eagerly as they laugh and play. Arab sages considered the symbolism behind this phenomenon which portrays the palm tree being pelted by stones and pebbles (effectively being abused), then repaying this offence by gifting its choicest ripe fruits. This is the origin of the parable we teach our youngsters so that they may understand life's multifaceted meanings and so that their souls may incline towards virtue and honourable morals.

> "Be like the palm trees, soaring above grudges –
> pelted with rocks only to return the choicest fruits."

> "Be patient when the gales of life frustrate you –
> For ease arrives only after hardship [the greatest storms]."

Even though I say so myself, this has always been my response to the unjust, aggressive abuse that I was subjected to and harm that I was caused. That is all water under the bridge; and those days have passed. Today, I cannot help but smile when I recall a few incidents in a long series of events during which the Egyptian diplomats unjustly showered me with rocks and pebbles, impudently and arrogantly trying their utmost to harm the Arab candidate for the post of UNESCO Director-General.

During that time, I recalled the wonderful piece written by Salah Jahin in the aftermath of the attack by Israel on 5 June 1967, condoling Egypt by wiping the defeat, humiliation and brokenness from her forehead and reminding Egyptians of their true nature. During my campaign for the UNESCO position, I felt the Egyptian diplomats were in a similar place; it was palpable that their living spirit had shrivelled – for nobody could be further than they were from the consciously dynamic Egyptian existence.

The results of the first round emerged. It was a round in which most candidates voted and where I ranked first place. Subsequently, it was obvious that I was the voters' favourite and it seemed as if events were, in fact, moving towards the election of an Arab as the head of UNESCO, six whole decades after its establishment. At this point, the Egyptian diplomats moved to reverse the tide of events and sought to ambush me, lobbying against me after I had garnered the most votes, and launching a joint media campaign with the Kingdom of Saudi Arabia and the United Arab Emirates against me.

Everyone knows what took place on the morning of 5 June 2017, when some of our neighbouring countries announced that they were severing relations with the State of Qatar and began to impose an unjust blockade that prevented our air and sea lines from crossing their territorial airspace and waters. All this under the pretext of accusing us of co-operation with Iran and with terrorist groups. The UAE had preceded this announcement by hacking the Qatar News Agency's website in order to broadcast false information purportedly made by the Emir of the State of Qatar, which was conjured up in the darkened bunkers of Abu Dhabi and had nothing whatsoever to do with reality. And because a liar usually ends up believing their own falsehood, this blockading country demanded the closure of Al Jazeera's satellite channels as one of its 13 demands that were more risible than anything else. Despite all the criticisms levelled at it from all sides, the international community's belief in Al Jazeera and their confidence in the credibility of all its platforms and various languages put paid to the UAE's lies. Not to mention that Al Jazeera remained a critical primary source of news, to the extent that Hillary Clinton stated that she relied on Al Jazeera for news on the Arab world whilst she was in charge of the US Foreign Office.

To return to the malicious plot, I had thought that my deep love for Egypt and her people, as well as my long-term association with this country, would surely gain the Egyptian delegation's support. In fact, this is what the Egyptian emissary promised when he visited me in Doha. Sadly, the truth showed that Egypt's repeated failures in previous UNESCO elections caused the Egyptian Foreign Office to decide to attack any Arab candidate relentlessly. Instead of making an effort to support a fellow Arab, the Egyptian delegation proceeded to convince the ambassadors not to vote for me, especially the African ambassadors who had already decided to give me their voice, like His Excellency George Godia, the Kenyan ambassador to UNESCO. The Southern nations, especially the African countries, were firmly convinced that the Arab candidate would be their voice, defend their interests and work to restore the North/South equilibrium in the fields of education, culture and science. They had listened carefully to my programme and analysed its content at their leisure, focussing on initiatives that were aimed at rehabilitating young people and launching small-scale projects that would affect an immediate impact, for which I had already secured funding pledges from wealthy, highly conscientious individuals. At the end of the day, it was these initiatives that the Egyptian Foreign Minister sought to thwart in Africa, as well as in the countries of the Caribbean and Central America where the projects had been warmly welcomed and motivated these countries to commit to voting for the Arab candidate in his capacity as the bearer of these projects.

The relentless campaign was not restricted to officials but spilt over into the realm of the media, which tore away at people's honour in ways that would shame even those who profess to have no principles. As Arabs and Muslims, we learn and are taught never to resort to profanity during arguments. This is borne out by the fact that previous disagreements between various Gulf states never reached the stage where the honour of tribes, women and offspring were cursed, because both sides considered this to be an unconscionable abomination that those with honour and dignity would never dare to attempt even though their interests and points of view may differ. However, the law of the jungle overcame the activities of some media professionals and pushed them to slander freely, for example accusing my tribe of terrorism when everyone knows that the Bu Kawwara have no relationship – whether near or far – with terrorism in any shape or form. Not content with slander, they proceeded with mocking statements such as the one claiming that my appearance was that of an Iranian and not an Arab!

This suppressed hatred reached its climax when it exploded openly in front of everyone on the international scene. What the large delegation accompanying the Egyptian Foreign Minister in Paris had previously kept hidden now became evident when, on the day of the final vote, an uncouth person shouted madly in the corridors, yelling; "Down with Qatar, down with Qatar – Vive la France!"; thus prompting the security agents to remind him of the need to respect his own position and abide by diplomatic protocol. Perhaps the most appropriate response was that of our ambassador to UNESCO, Ali Zainal, who said in front of everybody: "Long live Egypt, long live Qatar; and long live all the Arab nations."

I thought deeply about what happened in that moment from the perspective of an intellectual as well as a politician and I was appalled by the way in which politics poisoned the wellspring of our morals, from which we drink. It dawned on me that the filth of politics had caused all standards of virtue to be discarded into the Red Sea. I do not know why, at that very moment, an image of Machiavelli in his book *The Prince* occurred to me as he presents reasons for the justification of seizing power and wielding it in any way as long as it seeks to achieve the intended goal, regardless of whether or not it is ethical. I wondered – what credibility remained to those who trampled roughshod over morals and ethics whilst professing to believe in both divine and human principles? I then felt that the road towards establishing a new morality was still nascent and overlong; and that we, in the Arab region, still suffer from a scarcity of this morality to the extent that we are still building individuals prior to building cities, in the words of our ancient Arab philosophers.

I thank God that I am not easily fazed by pointless arguments, and I would view these scenes with a sardonic smile on my face and verses of French poetry running through my mind – I recalled

Alfred de Vigny and his poem "The Death of the Wolf", in which he proclaims: "Silence, alone, is noble – the rest is all vanity and weakness."[1] But I discovered the dangerously low level to which some Arab officials' values had sunk.

Lebanon – the Cracked Mirror

My relationship with Lebanon was established in the 1970s, when I was Qatari Charge d'Affaires in Beirut and my admiration for its cultural and political pluralism has only continued to increase over the years. Given my long history with Lebanon, my love for her people and my close relationship with her successive governments, I was convinced, based on events that had taken place since the start of my campaign, that the Lebanese vote would be one in my favour when we reached the final rounds. A few weeks after my candidacy was announced, the Lebanese Prime Minister, Tammam Salam had visited and enthusiastically assure me of Lebanon's support – throughout the two days he spent with me in Doha, most of our conversation revolved around UNESCO and its future. However, surprises followed shortly thereafter, when I learned that Lebanon would nominate its own candidate for this international position, Vera El Khoury. The then Lebanese Minister of Culture came specially to Doha to inform me that Lebanon would be putting forward a candidate for the post of UNESCO Director-General, and that this candidate would withdraw in my favour should it transpire that their chances of success were slim. As a result, a rumour emerged to the effect that Lebanon intended to present a candidate of extremely high calibre who would compete seriously for the post – none other than Ghassan Salameh, a university graduate who knew the ins and outs of politics and was well versed in international relations and cultural diplomacy due

---

1 Alfred de Vigny : La mort du loup (Seul le silence est grand, tout le reste est faiblesse).

to his intimacy with intellectual circles in France. It then became clear that there were regional parties who were encouraging him to run, assuring him of their willingness to endorse him politically and support him financially.

I do not pretend to hide my disquiet at these repeated events, for the Beirut which I knew was not the same Beirut from which these announcements came thick and fast – I was astonished, for how could one such as myself, an admirer of Lebanese valour and creativity, ever forget the Beirut whose university embraced me during my studies after my time in Cairo?

Beirut remained deeply within me, this wonderful civilisation that Mahmud Darwish wrote so lovingly and deeply about on the eve of his departure: "The soul in a mirror, embodied." In Beirut, I learnt the art of living and came to love this pure, transparent city; just as I was amazed by the Lebanese entrepreneurial work ethic, inherited along with sailors' daring and an adventurous spirit from their ancestors. This is what made the pain so intensely acute – it was a friend stabbing me in the back in my hour of need. Finally, the Lebanese officially nominated Vera El Khoury instead of Ghassan Salameh as a result of internal political dynamics, only to discover that this was a mistake as their candidate received a meagre three votes in the first round.

I still believe that Lebanon deserved better than this; and they would have attracted more votes had they chosen the academic Ghassan Salameh, veteran intellectual and consummate international networker. Despite this, I could not be certain that he had the potential to succeed, since a UNESCO Director-General requires substantially solid financial and political support from their country, which Lebanon was unable to offer at the time facing, as it did, considerable social upheaval and a severe financial crisis. After all of this, I learned that Lebanon voted for me in the third and fourth rounds, and the Lebanese UNESCO representative promised to stand by my side in the final round. However, to my astonishment,

I discovered that he was not present on polling day. I asked about this and the response I received was meaningless humming and hawing. On the day of the decisive vote, I witnessed the UNESCO delegate being replaced by Lebanon's Ambassador to France, Rami Adwan, who was appointed directly by the Minister of Foreign Affairs to vote in that particular round. Things went awry and moral values fell into relapse once again. It seemed to me that our Arab culture was afflicted by a crisis of values and that intellectuals were inclined to indulge their political whims and desires in the absence of elevating authentic values.

France – a Total Eclipse

I lived for decades in France when I was the Qatari ambassador in Paris, and while I was there, God blessed me with my son Imran. It was the city where he grew up alongside his elder brother Tamim and his sister Iman. The charm of the City of Light and the metropolis of French culture is lost on no-one. I am proud of the legacy I left in the French capital when I collaborated with a group of Arab ambassadors to establish the Arab World Institute as a bridge facilitating exchanges, a fertile space enriching constructive intellectual dialogue between Arab culture and Western culture in general and French culture in particular. As a diplomat, I have woven a network of relationships with many personalities from the worlds of politics, media, culture, philosophy and the arts. Here, I acknowledge that France reciprocated my respect and appreciation, for I was awarded the highest state recognition at the hands of three presidents of different political persuasions: Valéry Giscard d'Estaing, who presented me with the National Order of Merit, François Mitterrand, who awarded me the Légion d'Honneur medal and François Hollande, the Ordre des Arts et des Lettres.

Despite all legitimate criticisms of the French state, especially of its colonial past, I have also witnessed the honourable stances taken by French intellectuals, writers, artists and many French politicians on behalf of the countries of the South and their sincere, spirited struggle for the rights of the oppressed in impoverished countries and in former French colonies. I believed that France valued every intellectual that was committed to their cause; and I saw a higher purpose in my candidacy to UNESCO and a true commitment to a lofty ambition. I recalled situations where free intellectuals risked their lives for the sake of a just cause. I remembered Émile Zola when he published his historical letter: "J'Accuse...!", the painful exile Victor Hugo was subjected to as a result of his stance and I also thought of Jean-Paul Sartre who believed in the commitment of an intellectual to a cause, embodied by selling the banned newspaper *La Cause du peuple* in front of the Renault factory in Boulogne-Billancourt, the symbolic prison of the French working class.

I appreciated the UN's francophone message, along with its dissemination in French, as a means by which the countries of the South can make their voices heard and defend their rights on the international stage. As Minister of Culture, Heritage and Arts, this was one of the reasons that prompted me to work for the State of Qatar to become a member of UN, which took place in 2013. There is wisdom in the French proverb that cautions against "throwing the baby out with the bathwater", or as we say in our Arab culture; "What has been mostly spoilt should not be entirely discarded." Doha has benefitted from French culture as evidenced by the presence of more than one French institute, including the Voltaire Institute and the Bonaparte Institute, which reveal new horizons for our youth and the upcoming generations in order that they may be more open to Western culture in general.

Thanks to my intimate knowledge of Paris and its international intellectual and political circles, I was comfortable with the presence of the UN headquarters there, so I devoted the last few months in the run up to the elections to staying in my Parisian home and managing my campaign by maintaining communication with delegates from various UN member countries and focusing in particular on the member states of the Executive Council who were legally authorised to vote. On the other hand, I knew full well that I was on my French rival Audrey Azoulay's home ground, that she was following my campaign closely and I had no doubt that an invitation to meet her was probably a strategic move on her part. Was she curious to see her adversary, whose campaign the press dubbed "bulldozing" up close? Or was she trying to send a message to the media insinuating the possibility of a clandestine agreement between us, the threads of which were being woven behind the scenes? Perhaps she was not hostile towards the Arab candidate, knowing that the international stage was convinced 2017 would be the Arabs' turn as they had never once had the opportunity to oversee UNESCO since it was formed? These questions swirled round my mind when we met – a simple meeting according to protocol in which Azoulay expressed her appreciation for my sporting spirit and for the transparent nature of my campaign before the media took a photograph of this occasion.

As days passed, the glittering image I had of the French Republic began to gradually fade away and darkness began to spread over Paris, the City of Light, home to human rights and freedom of expression until, for me, France's light was dimmed and her candle snuffed out. It seemed to me that France in this age of enlightenment betrayed her own renaissance and was now transformed into a biddable tool in the hands of people who had no real connection to the lofty ideals upon which human rights are founded. I became even more convinced that critique of Western thought should continue because westerners' betrayal did not end with colonialism but continues with those practices that reflect the relationship that their elite has with other peoples and their cultures. Alongside this is the superiority that they believe they deserve, thus ensuring that relationships become entirely opportunistic, transactional and fickle rather than based on noble values.

French Media Sleepwalks into Disgracing the City of Light

Towards the end of his presidential term and whilst the final nominations were being submitted for the position of UNESCO Director-General, President Hollande nominated Azoulay to represent France in the elections. His decision gave rise to a strong wave of condemnation in the French media and political and cultural circles. An overwhelming sense of shame regarding this move rippled through France, for many considered it to be unsporting. Diplomatic norms and conventions prevent representatives of the UNESCO host country from being nominated for the post of Director-General, as they have additional access and powers at their disposal that are deemed unacceptable by other nations in their insistence in maintaining a level international playing. For the host nation to hold directorship of UNESCO would be tantamount to turning the entire organisation into a backroom for the French Ministry of Foreign Affairs to come and go as they please. According to the noises being made by other member nations from all around the world over the past few years, it appears that this is, in fact, what took place.

Despite this denunciation, both explicit and implicit, French media – usually known for its professional representation of the Fourth Estate – behaved as a propaganda machine would for another nation. During previous elections, the French press would give prominent coverage to candidates and their profiles, devoting a considerable number of pages to introducing them personally and providing them with a platform from which they could present their own vision and manifestos. However, the situation this time was entirely different, with the candidates barely granted a passing mention and the overwhelming majority of French coverage dedicated to biased content that was unabashedly pro-Azoulay. Puff pieces glorifying her were constantly churned out along with statements of blind support. Observers were disgusted by this, because they would have accepted it had the organisation's headquarters not been in France – then, French media would have the right to support its own candidate exclusively. But for France to host UNESCO and for its media to turn a blind eye to the ongoing elections? This was considered by everyone, and by the observers in particular, as most unbecoming of a nation credited with the establishment of human rights and freedom of expression.

If the French media had remained content with merely ignoring Azoulay's adversaries, perhaps this would have been excusable. To openly practice manipulation and deceit on the other hand, is another matter entirely and strongly indicates the absence of any moral compass, professional values, equal opportunities or any other universal principle that the Northern nations are so fond of bragging about. How can one accept being approached for interview by no less than four well-known French newspapers – namely, *Libération, Le Parisien, Le Journal du Dimanche* and *Paris-Normandie* – agreeing, dedicating the necessary time and effort to prepare; only to find no mention made whatsoever of the Arab candidate, despite promises that these interviews would be published directly before the elections? It is even stranger to note that each of these papers have very different political leanings. *Libération* is left-wing, whilst *Le Parisien* is right-wing; neither of which prevented them from blindly siding with a Northern nation against the countries of the South. Were we not in the land of freedom of expression and in a country that respects different points of view, encouraging plurality and diversity of opinion?

I remembered that unfortunately the French media often made many "concessions", sacrificing both the respect of their readership and the truth. Wasn't Bernard-Henri Lévy permitted to become a prominent stakeholder in *Libération* at a time when Laurent Jauffret, then editor-in-chief was fully aware of the accusations that surrounded him?

I had lived and worked in Paris for over half a century, yet never imagined that the media would, to this extent, move like a pack of wolves, casting aside every global principle, code of conduct or oath on which the profession of journalism is based.

A plethora of evidence exists, testifying to the high esteem in which I hold the freedom of the press in particular, and the freedom of opinion generally; one instance being that I was perhaps the only Minister of Information in the world who worked earnestly to shut down their own ministry in Qatar in 1997, sincere in the belief that there should not be a ministry that supervises or censors the media. I did not hesitate to establish the Doha Centre for Media Freedom in October 2008 with Sheikh Hamad bin Thamer Al Thani. It was the first centre of its kind in the Arab world, whose mission it is to defend journalists and to provide them with assistance in emergency situations. Furthermore, I regularly meet many journalists in Doha, including CEOs and editors-in-chief from prominent publications such as the New York Times and others. In fact, on a personal level, I am a member of the International Federation of Editors and continue to publish opinion pieces that have been translated into almost 10 languages.[1] How can someone who is an active member of the international media community accept or tolerate the intolerance and prejudice that manifested in the French press' behaviour? Was this not a betrayal, twice over, of the spirit of enlightenment?

---

1   See: Al-Kawari: Hamad bin AbdulAziz "It's Time to Reform the UN" 12th May 2020. Published in seven languages on the Project-syndicate website https://www.project-syndicate.org/commentary/united-nations-covid19-response-shows-need-for-reform-by-hamad-bin-abdulaziz-al-kawari-2020-05?barrier=accesspaylog

A Paradox Planted by Hollande along the Champs-Élysées

Previously, I mentioned my French adversary Azoulay's invitation, asking me to meet her. It transpired that this was intended purely as a photo opportunity for the media in order to portray an implicit truce between us regarding the post of the UNESCO Director-General when, in fact, the reality could not be further from the truth. It is worth noting that the French invitations always reached me via official channels, including an invitation I received from Aurélien Lechevallier, President Emmanuel Macron's diplomatic advisor, to meet in his office at the Élysée Palace. Lechevallier was later appointed as France's ambassador to South Africa. French media close to the ruling circles described Azoulay's nomination as an unwanted inheritance bequeathed by Hollande to Emmanuel Macron. The new president, freshly in post, could not therefore have the audacity to withdraw his support for her or to face down her supporters, no matter how few they might have been. In response to his invitation, I went to meet the president's advisor. I was imagining that he wanted to understand my stance more closely vis-à-vis the attempts of UNESCO's host country to steal the position from the Arab bloc with whom it had so many shared interests in different areas. In return, this meeting was an opportunity for me to express my point of view to decision makers in France. Fortunately, Aurélien Lechevallier was a good listener. In fact, he didn't speak much, and after the usual diplomatic niceties he contented himself with asking me what I thought of the French candidate, then proceeded to jot down my replies in his notebook.

I answered that, based on my code of conduct as a former diplomat, I had committed myself to refrain from criticising any fellow candidate during my campaign and to content myself with fighting my corner cleanly, without arguments and accusations. Then I took a step back and corrected myself in order to clarify my point of view, because his question was a direct one that left me no room for manoeuvre or compliments. "How can one understand – much less accept – that the host country completely disregards all diplomatic protocol and international conventions and pro-actively nominates one of its own officials to run dishonourably against all the other countries of the world to which it plays host? Such laxity and mismanagement not only detracts from UNESCO's credibility, but also reflects badly on France as host to UNESCO headquarters – almost 30% of whose permanent employees are French. Are you intending to turn an international organisation which embraces all the countries of the world into the French Foreign Ministry's back garden? Even if we were to accept your candidate chasing after an international post after her short stint as Minister of Culture in the previous president's cabinet, and that she wants to linger a while longer in the limelight; then this still constitutes an egregious infringement of the Arab bloc's right to assume office which has not been granted once since UNESCO was founded? And if France believes in the continuity of state, it should be noted that President Hollande promised to support my candidacy during an official visit to Doha in May 2015. So, has France suddenly decided to shirk its leaders' commitments and adopt the diplomacy of false promises whilst remaining a civilised, active country on the world stage that occupies a seat on the Security Council?

"Your government has all the necessary tools for evaluation; and you have only to look at the other candidates' manifestos to realise that I am the only one with a fully comprehensive plan for a new start for UNESCO that includes manually renovating the HQ's old buildings and renovating the organisation's entire infrastructure, as well as its digital networks, so that UNESCO can operate at the cutting edge of contemporary times. I have even found financial backers for these initiatives. I would like to add that my proposal also includes plans to hold cultural, educational and intellectual forums similar to Davos, which will bring together French intellectuals, prominent individuals and all major stakeholders in the fields of philosophy, culture and education to contribute towards their improvement in the hope that this will serve all humanity."

Lechevallier was listening intently, so I continued speaking, saying: "Seeing as how we are speaking frankly, and in the spirit of openness in which your invitation was extended, I will share a perspective that I wouldn't normally, had you not taken the initiative to reach out. Even if we overlook the host country's nomination of its own candidate, how are we to understand France's choice? France, a country replete with veteran individuals who are prominent in the fields of intellectual thought, culture and academic work – why would you not choose a member of this global elite? Why would this role be given to an inexperienced young employee whose portfolio only contains a brief stint as Minister of Culture on President Hollande's personal recommendation?"

Lechevallier visited Doha in March 2019 and expressed his wish to meet with me, so I responded to his request once more. From his words, I understood that he was aware of a book I was writing in order to document what had taken place during the campaign, so I took the opportunity to inform him that I would be making our conversation at the Élysée Palace public. His response was that he had nothing to hide and that freedom of expression was guaranteed. The conversation took a tangent, and I asked about the behaviour of the French press that had shocked me in this, the country of liberté. His answer was that the government does not interfere with the media's editorial choices. Politely, I smiled inwardly to myself remembering an Arabic saying that roughly translates as "having guilt written all over your face", and thinking, meanwhile, of the difference between the suppression of facts and the dissemination of fake news.

The Rock in my Life

In this battle, like many others that challenged me in life, I was never alone. God blessed me with a wife who is my rock and my safe space. Were it not for Umm Tamim, my work would never have been completed. No-one was as persevering or as encouraging as her. She is the one who stood by me, exhorting me to overcome all the challenges and obstacles in my way. The role she played in supporting me was no less than the many roles she played in our family and in raising our children, monitoring their education, guiding them morally and instilling the love of knowledge in them.

She remained detached from my work and never involved herself directly, contenting herself with being my source of moral support. She would always motivate me to aim higher and achieve more, as well as focus on our relationships with our relatives and friends. Despite all this, she was unjustly targeted and insulted by opponents, particularly those close to us, but she remained steadfast, exhorting me to focus on my work and leave small matters to little people.

In truth, Umm Tamim was my one companion during my life's journey in Paris, New York, Washington and most of the Arab world's capital cities. She is the one who accompanied me throughout my UNESCO campaign, an erudite and cultured lady who is well versed in the world surrounding her. In addition to being the wife of a diplomat and a minister and all that entails with regard to courtesy, taste and hospitality, she is an accomplished woman in her own right and a fine arts graduate with an extensive knowledge of literature, arts and culture. Moreover, it was she who brought up Iman, Tamim and Imran – international stars in their respective fields – whether in the world of business and finance, academia, or politics and diplomacy. Our children would not have managed to reach these prominent positions had they not learnt the value of principles, virtues, diligence and a stout work ethic at

Umm Tamim's hands. I spent all my life in service to my country, immersed in politics and diplomacy – my time did not stretch to overseeing their upbringing or monitoring their education. Were it not for the divine blessing that God had granted me in the person of Umm Tamim, they would have fallen victims to my preoccupation and single-minded focus on serving the nation at a time when Qatar desperately needed all its sons and daughters to rise and build its future; to lay foundations for its progress, development and modernity. We were all conscripted to serve this lofty goal.

Falling into a Culture War

Has Western hegemony finally shed its fig leaf? The West is well aware of the values of the people of the desert, even if its eyes are clouded by the Orientalist tendencies and colonialist perspectives that it has adopted for decades. The West – which has long believed and possibly continues to believe that its very 'Western-ness' is the model paradigm of civilisation in the history of humankind – often fails in the most basic of tests. However, this hurts the West more than it hurts us, because this contradicts and makes a mockery of the values that they parade but do not apply to others.

Here, I speak about the West in general, despite the fact that I was stung by Europe specifically; for the West unavoidably includes Europe, North America and other countries that are allied to European culture such as Australia and New Zealand – generally, the Christian world. However, I perceive the West as being cultures and practices that form a civilisational identity. I acknowledge that the world's major civilisations today revolve, in the main, around faiths, but I always see civilizations as more expansive entities and do not judge them based on the religions they are founded upon.

The West imposed its hegemony over centuries. Here, I recall the argument that Samuel Huntingdon posits as the reason for this: "The West has overcome the world not by religious, moral or intellectual superiority (to which few civilisations subscribed) but due to their upper hand in inflicting organised violence." This is a general overview of Western civilisation, but only a piece of the puzzle consisting of many precursors that led up to the West's superiority complex.

Decades ago, the German economist and sociologist Max Weber (1864 – 1920) compared the West with other civilisations and came to the conclusion that Western civilisation has exceptional advantages. The path it followed during the stages of its modern development was incomparable, enabling it to produce cultural values that do not exist in the East, including Chinese and Indic civilisations. He includes both rationality and a capitalist economic system among these as beneficiaries of scientific and technological development. These values were built into his treatise on religious, cultural and psychological incentives based on Protestant teachings, in order to portray Western culture as producing a modernity the like of which has never been witnessed.

Max Weber did not care as much about the Arab-Islamic civilisation as he did about the Chinese and Indic, but his writing left a trail for later thinkers who turned him into an icon of Western supremacy. Francis Fukuyama followed in his footsteps and called for the end of history, considering the Western civilisation to be the epitome of human civilisations; and that the world is witnessing the struggle of ideas and ideologies at its peak, with civilisation unable to continue after the West reaches the extreme stage of liberal democracy. He constantly equates the end of history with the end of the Western way of life, thus reducing contemporary human history to the history of Western progress only and perceiving the end of the Cold War as ushering in the beginning of the end. Doubtless, Fukuyama drew the concept of the end of history from Hegelian literature and revisited the conundrums of historical philosophy. However, he remained trapped between the millstones of Western philosophy that revolve around the West as the final iteration of civilisation!

Fukuyama continued to cling onto his thesis as the years passed, with the concept of the end of history evolving into an admission that Western democracy, along with its liberal culture and free economy, is the epitome of human development. This is not to mention the fact that the wars and conflicts in the Middle East, the Balkans or Afghanistan are nothing if not evidence that countries which do not subscribe to the liberal democratic ideal are doomed to the two-tailed whip of warfare and killing.

Thus, Fukuyama established his verdict on human societies: they are either advanced societies, revolving in the orbit of the Western capitalist system or backward societies doomed to ruin. Since Western culture is his prototype, he is quick to consider that this culture has a superior dimension that dominates all others. Therefore, he hypothesises that the globe can be divided into two worlds – an exemplary, advanced world; and a backward world that is incapable of progressing or moving on from the status quo unless they seek and latch onto Western modernity.

Fukuyama conceded that: "Power politics still prevail among countries that do not adopt liberal democracy. Relative delays in the arrival of industrialisation and nationalism to the Third World will lead to a marked difference between the behaviour of many Third World countries on one hand and the behaviour of industrial democracies on the other. In the foreseeable future, the world will be split into two – those who have overcome history and those who continue to drown in history."[1] Naturally, in his eyes, those who overcome history are the liberal West. As for the others, they remain has-beens in an ossified history. Fukuyama anticipates that a clash between these two worlds will be caused by two reasons: the

---

1   Francis Fukuyama, The End of History. Al-Ahram Centre for Translation and Publishing, Cairo, first edition, 1993, p 242

first, conflict over oil and the second, migration; where the world will witness a tsunami of migration from poorer, backward nations to the more prosperous ones.

This is how the world appears to one of the most important American thinkers, a historic world for developing countries and a post-historic, progressive world for secure Western countries. This division consolidates and embeds the concept of a clash between two worlds and has doubtless laid the groundwork for other theories promoting a "clash of civilisations" instead of dialogue, further marginalising those already marginalised and subjecting those already oppressed to further oppression.

This hostile rhetoric intensified with the rising popularity of Samuel Huntingdon's ideas, who exhumed Bernard Lewis' (1916 – 2018) ideas and reintroduced them into the public arena. This English orientalist was the first to coin the phrase "clash of civilisations" and conceptualise it, categorising the nature of conflict in the Middle East following the 1956 tripartite aggression against Egypt as a clash of civilisations, not a conflict between states and nations. He clung to this idea in most of his later theses in which he explained away the tensions between the Western world and the Islamic world as the inevitable result of this clash of civilisations.

Huntingdon did not veer much from his core hypothesis, constantly viewing the future of human history from this perspective and steering clear of any economic, political or military interpretation of existing conflict and considering civilisational and cultural factors to be the main catalysts igniting both present and future conflicts. Huntingdon chose a new attitude with regard to analysing global politics whilst relying on this element – in his opinion, politics will be defined by this clash of civilisations whether at an international or a local level; and nations should be categorised or classified according to their cultures and religions. He defined eight major civilisations, namely – Chinese civilisation, based on Confucianism, Japanese civilisation based on Shintoism,

Indic civilisation based on Hinduism, Islamic civilisation based on Islam, Western civilisation based on Judaism and Christianity, Eastern European civilisation based on Orthodox Christianity, Latin American civilisation based on Catholicism and African civilisation based on various local beliefs; relegating the latter to the very end of this list due to the many reservations he had regarding it. All these civilisations seek to defend themselves and strive to ensure their continued existence and perpetuity, however, in his eyes, they can never be compared to the Western civilisation that, at its very core is based on Greek logic, Roman jurisprudence, the separation of Church and State and on individual freedoms.

Although Huntingdon inaccurately depicts the basic features of most of these civilisations, he considers the Chinese and Arab-Islamic civilisations as ones that are incapable of divesting themselves from their defining characteristics and embracing integration with the project called Western civilisation. Thus, he classifies them both as adversarial civilisations, simultaneously in competition with the West and living in retreat. In fact, he believes that the Arab-Islamic civilisation is one that is hostile because it is based on violence, claiming that Christians and others unanimously agree that emerging wars and disputes that emerge along the borders of Islamic lands reflect an espousal of violence. In short, he holds that Islam itself nurtures the seed of violence and hostility vis-à-vis the Other!

This depiction and conclusion are astonishing because Huntingdon fails to explain the main concepts in the Arab-Islamic civilisation that result in violence, or even those within the Chinese civilisation, which he alludes has a motivation for expansion, domination and the accrual of power. When Huntingdon speaks of what he calls "the spirit of culture" that can be found in every civilisation, we cannot conceive of the presence of an innate germ of hostility and violence because the analysis of cultures cannot possibly resort to such a given. Such judgements invite statements such as "Western civilisation is the only civilisation that is innately endowed with what others are bereft of," – i.e. that it is pacifist and not based on violence, whereas others are! In speaking thus, Huntingdon further entrenches the idea that these civilisations are ossified and incapable of changing, developing with the times or evolving to fit in. He posits that they are "true to their core" – this is an extreme provocation to these cultures and a harsh sentence replete with ideologization served by a Western thinker with a superiority complex. Huntingdon passed away in 2008, yet it is as if his presence continues to live with us, in much the same way as he remained faithful to Bernard Lewis' main theses. "The clash of civilisations" is an oft-repeated slogan that lies at the core of many unjust Western theses and continues to nestle deep in the global psyche. Bernard Lewis' voice continues to reverberate loudly, saying: "The lands of Islam knew next to nothing about the European renaissance, the religious reform movement or the technological revolution, because they used to (and apparently still do) belittle those who lived beyond their Western borders, seeing them as barbarians who lived in the dark and considering them to be even more inferior than the Asian infidels in the East who were one degree more advanced, being at least in possession of beneficial skills and useful innovations whilst the Europeans had nothing." This verdict used to have a reasonable modicum of truth, then became obsolete as time went on and is now an imminent danger. [1]

These self-same provocations limit Huntingdon's discourse and seep into judgements issued by other Western thinkers who still subscribe to theories that revolve around "the clash of civilisations" and "the war of cultures". Unfortunately, most international organisations tend to occupy this orbit and are buffeted by slogans calling for dialogue just as they are swayed by delusions of superiority

---

1 Bernad Lewis, Western influence and Muslim reactions, tr. Muhammad Enany, foreword and introduction Raouf Abbas, Sutur magazine p6

and the vanquishing rhetoric of Western supremacy as a model for human civilisation. These disturbances do not only impact the world order as a whole but permeate through to a much more basic level – one where decisions are taken within the most prominent international organisation that calls for intercultural dialogue – thus reflecting the torturous route trodden towards making these slogans come alive, before ultimately, they fail.

A Personal Test – Diametrically Opposed to Accepting the Other

Let us examine these ideas as manifestations in reality, and take, by way of example, an incident in which I was directly involved. The 2017 elections for UNESCO Director-General exposed many of the frustrations that were hidden in Western culture generally, revealing the hollowness of empty slogans that were paraded in front of humanity in the form of higher principles, which necessitated the Arab bloc in UNESCO accepting this result unwillingly, under any circumstances. In this moment, I realised that the civilisational construct in which we live will never do justice to the countries of the South but will actively promote legislation that causes unequal opportunities to take root, despite calls for its abolition.

This is how the countries of the North turned their backs on equality, trust and human dignity, for all weapons – both legitimate and otherwise – were used to derail the Arab candidate as he approached the finishing line during the last round of elections to be UNESCO Director-General. Here, the motive was not to excise a person of Arab culture and heritage alone, but to move the countries of the South in general well away from circles of leadership in an organisation that would have had great influence and authority across the world, had it moved earnestly on its new path towards reform. What calmed my soul and made me proud, despite the Northern nations' egregiously unprincipled behaviour, was the enthusiasm, support and change in public opinion that I witnessed and followed across the Arab countries, South America and the African continent after the results of each of the first four rounds.

People in most of the Southern nations and remote areas were glued to their television sets or to the internet, eagerly following the election proceedings, willing one of their own representatives to win the UNESCO leadership. The circle of dreams which they could legitimately hope for widened when they witnessed their candidate proceed through the first four rounds; and their enthusiasm intensified directly proportionate to adversaries' and competitors' frustrations. Because of this this, I do not absolve those Arabs whom I had considered to be my nearest and dearest from the charge of aiding and abetting this, for had it not been for their betrayal, the West would never have achieved its goal. That is why it is only fair that we must shoulder the consequences of our actions as Arabs.

The election process moved in many dishonest, guilty ways through which enmity to Arab civilisation found its mark. I was on the verge of making millions of peoples' dreams come true, had it not been for the fearsome covenant between those with a Western superiority complex and those from our own flesh and blood who allowed narrow personal interests to overcome their support for the truth. Despite my honourable exit from the melee of elections, I continue this journey till this very day. I looked forward to revealing some of the hitherto untold situations and practices – some secret, some public – in this book. I resolved to uncover the practices of an internationally accultured elite who betrayed their own principles and were shown by events to be incapable of restoring equilibrium to North-South relationships in a just manner according to the principles upon which UNESCO was founded.

What happened goes far beyond my own person and reaches every intellectual who cares about and is committed to humanitarian causes. There was not a single day that passed where I felt I was representing myself as much as I believed that I was articulating the words of those without as voice. As for the status quo, in which the Arab candidate's victory was snatched during the throes of an explosive campaign, it has demonstrated the limits of the elite's thinking and has allowed the conspiracies that caused it to be known by all. It exposed those who strove to deny all new talent hailing from developing countries who possessed both the sincere intention and the creative ability to compete on an equal footing with those who have monopolised the world's fate over the past few centuries.

Against this current — and despite the scheming of this fake elite — I met with these very talents who hailed from the Southern nations and I became closely acquainted. I found them to be extremely capable, competent and resolute in a way that I had not witnessed in the elites who dominate the world stage. Here, I realised was a latent opportunity that must be protected from extinction at all costs until the time arises once again for the election of a new UNESCO Director-General. Perhaps then the UN will benefit from the experiences and outlooks of talented people in order to work sincerely according to its principles in disseminating education, culture and the sciences.

What took place during the campaign between 2016 and 2017 represented a rendezvous with history that many adversaries and certain brothers had wished would not take place. They all failed to understand that an Arab diplomat at UNESCO's helm for the first time since its establishment would strengthen multilateral international co-operation in the service of humanity and would work to remind everyone of our shared destiny, as well as extend solid bridges between the Arab-Islamic civilisation and the other civilisations of the world without discrimination, whether historically or in the future. Those who were openly hostile and strove to cut me loose deliberately forgot that this Arab diplomat would stop at nothing and would give his all to breathe life into this organisation that was established to bring all the world's nations together.

Nonetheless, what took place was beneficial in that it motivated me to revisit my stance towards – and my perception of – European cultural history specifically and Western cultural history in general. As a result of this experiment, I came to know that Europe's multifaceted, often contradictory history throws a long shadow over our present; for Europe is not only about artistic renaissance, the age of enlightenment, musical heritage, sophisticated architecture, modernist poetry and philosophy that produced existential ideas and elevated modern thought, no. Europe is also religious and nationalistic extremism, racist ideology, colonialist history and supremacist beliefs and ideologies. This history is replete with contradictions that cannot remain on the bookshelves of the past, it moves with Europe's stances and manifests itself whenever it is tested with communicating with other civilisations.

Building Bridges, not Barriers

In order to counterbalance what is happening in our current time, it is incumbent upon us, and our youth specifically, to discover all there is in our expansive world. Instead of erecting separatist barriers, we must strive towards building and extending bridges that connect humankind, between religions and faiths and between the global North and the global South. This is the horizon to which every free, impartial intelligent person, who rises above petty, temporal personal gains aspires towards. That is why I have always fought for this throughout my life, whether during my time as an ambassador in Paris, a student and diplomat in New York in the corridors of the Security Council or as a Minister for Culture, Arts and Heritage in my home country, and I have never veered away from this path. Hand on my heart when I say it is this conviction, deep in my soul, that drove me to submit my candidacy in 2017 for the post of Director General of UNESCO.

This mission was never just an aspiration, but a goal I actively pursued. It led me to visit and tour more than 60 countries in four different continents. I would extend bridges between cultures, with the images of barriers that had been erected by humans in bygone eras playing in my mind and motivating me to continue, so that we may have hope!

Since the time of our prophet Ibrahim Al Khalil (Allah's beloved), may peace be upon him, barriers greater than five metres in height and more than 90 kilometres in length were being constructed in order to protect the Royal Library in Nineveh; as if to prevent the Other from having access to knowledge so that only one single race may have sole rights to it to the exclusion of all others. Barrier after barrier continued to be erected throughout the world to separate one group from another, to define geographical, cultural and political boundaries in order to exclude, 'other-ise' and create enemies. Building continued apace until the Berlin Wall – the "Wall of Walls" – came crashing down with thunderous consequences in November 1989.

This was no more than the inevitable outcome of the collapse of the Eastern Bloc and was much vaunted and celebrated by the majority of the world. It seemed to everyone that this symbolic and somewhat romantic event was the death knell for the Cold War between the capitalist West led by the United States and the Warsaw Pact led by the former Soviet Union.

Perhaps the justifications that called for the construction of these walls – wherever they are built – may appear logical from a certain perspective, for it is assumed that they constitute a protection against illegal immigration, terrorism, international or regional conflicts and ethnic or religious confrontations; but on the other hand, they isolate poverty and misery, hermetically sealing them away from the vision of those who are sufficiently privileged to live a comfortable life in societies of abundance. Furthermore, they constitute an infringement on human rights in that they prevent freedom of movement, prompting certain European politicians to state that they do not accept their countries becoming the world's dumping ground – as if there are pure citizens of the world and others who are deemed impure. Truth be told, we note that until today, building barriers continues to be far easier than removing them, especially among those populists who hold power. In fact, plans to erect separatist, isolationist walls have returned with a vengeance. Extortionate budgets have been allocated to this, escalating exclusionist tendencies and deepening isolation, intolerance and rejection of the Other.

The Tale of the Two Brothers' Wall

Our collective memory is replete with stories about building walls throughout human history, equally counterbalanced by a rich heritage of stories detailing the wisdom behind extending bridges. Amongst these is the following traditional folk tale from the Arab world:

It is said that a man was living with his family on the banks of a river. He owned fruitful orchards that provided him with a comfortable life, and his brother lived on the opposite riverbank under similar circumstances. As the days passed, they began to bicker over land ownership and the movement of their flocks from one bank to the other in search of pasture and to graze. In time, the elder brother travelled to distant lands far from his family in order to trade. So, the younger brother decided to build a wall along the riverbank to create a barrier between him and his brother and to prevent his brother's sheep and cows from trespassing onto his land. Accordingly, he made his way to the village where there lived a skilled builder who was also renowned for his wisdom, and he asked him to build a wall that would keep him and his brother apart. The wise builder agreed on the condition that the younger brother should not interfere in his work until he was completely finished with the job he was commissioned to do. The builder then took himself to a hut that he owned in the forest which he kept for the purpose of drying large logs that were used as pillars in construction. He picked out the strongest, most solid logs that were widest in diameter. The next day, he carried the logs to the edge of the riverbank. Then he took them to the middle of the deep river and drove them deeply into the riverbed to ensure that they were embedded securely. He arranged these logs into two parallel lines and during the next few days, he tied connections between each pillar. Once this was achieved, he proceeded to cover the horizontal surface with broad wooden planks until a solid bridge was formed over the water, connecting both banks. He devoted the last days of his work to adorning the bridge with beautiful carvings and decorative works of art, whilst the younger brother looked on in astonishment at what the wise man was doing, unable to question him because of his promise. As fate would have it, the elder brother returned from his travels on the very same day that the builder was finishing his work. He looked at the beautiful bridge that connected his riverbank with the opposite side; and saw his brother monitoring the work being done. The elder brother felt a rush of delight and pleasure, because he believed that his brother had undertaken to connect the two riverbanks so that the family could communicate easily without the onerous water-crossing. He rushed to embrace his brother, kiss him, and thank him for what he had done. The younger brother felt the sweetness and warmth of brotherhood and felt ashamed of his original intentions, having initially demanded that the wise man build a wall of separation.

Thus, affection, intimacy and the brotherly connection between them was re-established. Before taking his leave, the wise man turned to them saying: "Yes, you were both in need of this bridge that would connect rather than separate you from each other. Henceforth, there will be no estrangement between brothers as of today."

In the same manner, we see the affluent societies in our times erect one barrier after another so they can monopolise the world's bounties and resources and deprive others of them. Political, economic, cultural, social and even ethnic isolation have become core demands for populist parties that feed on the misery of others whilst claiming to protect the "zones of prosperity" exclusively for the use of the rich and powerful.

One of the strange paradoxes of our time is that these material walls continue to be built higher and higher, yet we live in an era of globalisation and all that entails in terms of communication over the ether and interhuman connections. A simple internet connection is all that is required for a citizen of one country to communicate with the citizens of the world indiscriminately, regardless of any differences in gender, race or otherwise.

An indication that barriers rather than bridges are being built is in the interest that writers have for the topic. In his novel "The Wall", British author John Lanchester predicts the very real disasters that threaten the world as a result of an ever-encroaching separationist culture and expresses his opposition to this culture of barriers that multiple politicians in the West are enamoured of, believing everyone has the right to live in security, safe from danger.

Or, as Muslims would say: "There's space for all on God's Earth."

In 1961, the residents of Berlin woke one day to be confronted with the reality of a wall being built through the middle of their capital city, dividing it into western and eastern halves; bisecting its neighbourhoods, main roads and smaller streets — to the extent that it actually some split homes in two so that the garden became part of East Berlin and the rest of the house stayed in West Berlin. This wall separated friends and lovers from each other; and hundreds of thousands died attempting to flee from the eastern camp to the western side as a result of the totalitarian regime's oppression. The wall became a ribbon of death and a place of pain, separation and division.

There is no doubt that 1989 was the most significant year in world history since 1945 as it changed everything at the level of global politics, leading to the end of the Cold War, the collapse of communism in Europe and the fall of the Soviet Union. It enabled the unification of Germany and flung the doors open for a historically unprecedented European Union extending from Lisbon to Tallinn, NATO expansion, two decades of American supremacy, globalisation and the rise of Asia. Yet the only thing that the fall of the Berlin Wall did not change was politicians' continued obsession with erecting walls!

That is why this tragedy is repeated today, so that history repeats itself with perhaps one difference only, which is that the peoples of the Eastern Bloc migrate towards spaces that are culturally and ideologically similar to theirs – i.e, the West in general. But globalisation has, so to speak, "completely scattered the deck of cards", as if it saw humans as a race only, with no distinction or discrimination. Therefore, it is logical and to be expected that large numbers of people will flee from impoverished, marginalised and oppressed regions – that is, the old colonies – to more affluent countries in search of human dignity, or even sometimes simply in order to survive.

On the 20th of July 2019, three months before the date celebrating the 30th anniversary of the Berlin Wall's fall, the world celebrated the 50th anniversary of the first human steps taken on the surface of the moon. In July 1969, having been selected as commander of the Apollo 11 spacecraft, Neil Armstrong would be in the Eagle landing module as it alighted on the moon's surface before disembarking, so that this foot would be the first human touch to fall on the surface of this satellite that accompanies our planet around the sun. A magical moment indeed, if we were only to contemplate deeply and fully appreciate its significance. In the words of Armstrong himself: "That's one small step for man, one giant leap for mankind", a phrase that would be repeated infinite times in all the languages of the world. But his oft-forgotten colleague Michael Collins, who stayed in the Apollo 11 spaceship, was able to see the moon's surface from his vantage point orbiting the satellite every 50 minutes for 21 hours. To him, the moon appeared dusty and grey whereas our blue planet's light shone forth from afar. This Earth, this great sphere that is both our place of residence and our refuge, that reaches out indiscriminately to embrace everyone with not an ounce of prejudice. Indeed, she is home to all humanity and there is, truly, space for all on God's wide earth.

Chapter Two
Striving to Restore the Balance Between East and West

It seems to me that the words of the German poet Goethe: "To God belongs the Orient! To God belongs the Occident! North and South rest in peace between His hands", which resounded so forcefully more than 200 years ago, have now lost their potency in real life. The salient features of this universal vision for humanity have all but dissipated and are now replaced by an intensified compartmentalisation of the world. As the balance between the globe's two polar opposites begins to fade after two World Wars, the earth is now divided into North and South according to the criteria of those who are powerful and dominant.

A Deep Chasm

The disparity between wealthy nations and other, poorer or developing nations led to the emergence of the terminology "countries of the North" and "countries of the South" in the 1970s. This became embedded in 1980 in a report prepared by the German advisor Willy Brandt for the World Bank, entitled "North-South: A Programme for Survival",[1] later known simply as "The

---

[1] Willy Brandt, North-South: A Programme for Survival", A report by the Independent Commission for International Developmental Issues, tr. Zakaria Nasr, Sultan Abu Ali and Jalal Amin, published by The Kuwaiti Development Fund, Kuwait 1981

Brandt Report" which became a global reference describing the chasm between wealthy, mostly colonialist nations and developing or poorer nations, the majority of which were ex-colonies. These two disparate worlds were not sorted geographically, for the Brandt Line is no more than an illusion of territorial division, whereas the main criteria for division are the industrial and economic superiority of certain nations at the expense of others. This division is not spared the symbolic burden of Western supremacy that flourished during the nineteenth century and became manifest in military colonialist campaigns alongside accompanying claims of "the White race's" superiority over the "savage" nations. This view became enshrined within the North-South discourse also. That is why a strange paradox prevailed over the relationship between the North and the South, embodied in the Northern nations' claim that they alone possess a set of noble, refined human principles and values such as justice, equality, solidarity and the support for universal human rights; whereas in reality the only principles we observe translated into action are those that are attributed to the realms of barbarism, domination, extortion and the law of the jungle. Here, the strong prey on the weak without pity and devour them mercilessly.

The end of the Cold War did not usher in a new global phase that would help heal the nations so grievously wounded by colonialism. Instead, "…the end of the Cold War between the East and the West led to the beginnings of a borrowed war between the North and the South, so that two separate, contradictory and warring worlds were born. The first of these was the developed world, that of the North, which takes the form of a peremptory empire commanding and forbidding, and the second is the backward world, that of the South. The North looks askance at this world, regarding her children as nouveaux barbarians reminiscent of those the Roman Empire vanquished between the third and fourth centuries CE." [1]

The new world order emerged, with the old colonialist stance still running through its veins. The glittering slogans proclaiming human rights could not mask or hide its ferocity in dealing with weak peoples, nor did they find an arena where they could be put into practice outside the domain of industrially developed countries. These countries strove to implement democracy, social justice and lofty human principles within the borders of Northern countries only, i.e. within the Empire; whilst the rest of the world did not receive their share of these impractical or "realpolitik"[2] slogans that were adopted by the new world order. This, in my view, is a malicious recipe concocted to silence the human conscience and sort nations into peoples in possession of complete human dignity and others who cannot rise or aspire toward such lofty ideals as the concept of equality between the children of Adam. This is the contemporary manifestation of the master-slave narrative.

According to this division, the countries of the North shamefully occupied most of the positions in international organisations. Their elite did not break away from political circles, but rather acquiesced to this unfair political and economic division, preventing any Southern nation from holding a position of power or influence unless it came about as a response to pressure or in order to silence any dissenting voice from the Southern nations that world public opinion might follow. One of the most shocking paradoxes is the stranglehold

---

1   9 Abdullah AlDa'im "The New Barbarians? Will the sons of the Third World become the barbarians of the New World Order? Al-Mustaqbal Al-Arabi magazine, number 160 July 1992
2   In its Political Philosophy section, the British Encyclopedia defines Realpolitik "as policies based on practical goals and not on lofty ideals." Here, Realpolitik refers to a pragmatic outlook, far from distractions and disregarding ethical considerations. Realpolitik in diplomacy is usually associated with the relentless and realistic pursuit of national interests.

that certain nations hold over prominent and influential positions. These nations are infamous for their persecution of minorities and silencing human rights activists yet occupy these posts and are the most vociferous in demanding justice and equality!

A disturbing testimony to this is that the United Nations Secretariat, which gathers all the countries of the world in its plenary session, and the League of Nations before it have never – since they were founded in 1918 and 1947 respectively – had a Secretary General from the Islamic world, home to 1.5 billion people. As usual, Europe has been given the lion's share; with eight Secretaries-General out of 13. In order, they are Eric Drommund, a Brit; Joseph Avenol, a Frenchman; the Irishman Seán Lester; then another Brit, Hubert Gladwyn Jebb as an interim holder; Trygve Lie from Norway; Dag Hammarskjöld from Sweden; the Austrian Kurt Waldheim; and the current incumbent, António Guterres from Portugal. Even if an Arab took on this mantle once (Boutros Boutros-Ghali), there is not a single Muslim name to be found in the entire list, stretching over 100 years! As for UNESCO, the mantle of Director General has not been taken on by an Arab even once from the moment it was founded till our present time. In fact, the entire Arab bloc in the Executive remains wronged to this day, given that not a single one of their candidates has been accepted.

The Mirage of Diversity

As international organisations hold the banner of diversity aloft, it becomes apparent that the United Nations – and all its constituent bodies – suffers from a dearth in diversity, as mentioned in the statistics-based *Foreign Policy* circular. Claiming to support diversity policies has now become somewhat of a prevalent myth, a nebulous saying that reached the organisation well after it reached the Northern nations themselves; as for example, the Western nations themselves have a sorry record when it comes to diversity and did not even attempt to adopt diversity policies until they were pressured to do so by minorities who cherished their right to remain different.

If diversity requires recognition of the Other and their rights in full, then this "Other" who is not Western and does not belong to industrially developed countries will be nothing more than a word in the organisation's literature – a fact confirmed by Colum Lynch's article entitled: "The UN Has a Diversity Problem. Westerners are Overrepresented in Senior Positions across the World Body".[1] The UN employs 2,531 employees of American nationality, ie 6.75% of the total number of the organisation's employees – a percentage higher than that of any other country in the world. The United Kingdom, France, Italy and Spain also have the lion's share in comparison with other countries when taking their relative populations into consideration. Senior, prominent and highly paid jobs at the United Nations headquarters in Geneva and New York are reserved for Western countries, whilst the citizens of other countries are posted in field jobs in conflict zones such as the Democratic Republic of Congo and Mali. It gets worse at the UN headquarters in New York, as the numbers all lean one way; with 71% of jobs taken by citizens of Western countries and at least 90% of staff in certain units and departments, including the Policy Unit and the Strategic Communications Unit, are all Westerners.

The Director General António Guterres lamented the lack of representation from the Southern nations amongst UN staff, saying that we would be deluded to believe that we now lived in a post-apartheid world. In the Office for the Co-ordination of Humanitarian Affairs, for example, the institution has been led

---

[1] Colum Lynch's article in Foreign Policy, 16th October 2020:
"The UN Has a Diversity Problem. Westerners are overrepresented in senior positions across the world body.
https://preignpolicy.com/202/10/16/un-diversity-problem-workforce-western-ocha/

exclusively by British directors for the past 13 years, four of whom have been consecutive, direct appointments, without any sort of recruitment mechanism being activated. In fact, not only were they directly appointed in the absence of any competition, but they were also all former British politicians. United Nations staff also denounce the absolute monopoly British This will ensure that I have on senior posts in the organisation to the exclusion of all others.

Faced with these disparities and the vast difference between the utopian slogans about diversity and our racist, exclusionary reality , I was constantly striving; enlightened by my own experience as well as the experiences of free intellectuals and writers who believed in human dignity and were in solidarity with the causes of the peoples of the South. As Frantz Fanon, who remains an inspiration to all who struggle for the sake of freedom and dignity, would say: "I want one thing; and that is the end of man's enslavement of man, as well as the end of the other's enslavement of me. This will ensure that I find out and discover man, wherever he is."

A Continuous Quest

In my election manifesto for the position of Director-General of UNESCO, I sought - as any astute observer would not have failed to notice – to propose precise criteria necessary for the restoration of some semblance of balance between the countries of the North and the countries of the South, and a narrowing of the chasm between what people call the "mainstream" and the "margins". I was enthusiastic about the possibility of dialogue between the North and South. I always found the political movements that were witness in the 1970s to be a symbolic justification for the possibility of resurrecting meaningful dialogue, for the French premier Giscard d'Estaing's call for dialogue between the North and South in 1974 was no mere scream into a vacuum. It had consequences at the time, including a

United Nations General Assembly declaration on working towards establishing a new world order based on justice, equality, integration, unity and the common good between all nations during its 29th session, in addition to the convening of the conference "Dialogue between North and South" in Paris. Unfortunately, these efforts did not culminate in positive results and ended up in a dead end. Despite this, I continue to cling to d'Estaing's call, but it is in need of genuine activists and those loyal to its ideals.

Believing in the necessity of restoring dialogue, I devoted most of my field visits to countries of the South in Africa, Asia, Latin America and the Caribbean islands, listening to their problems and thinking of solutions that would drive them towards growth and development, especially in the education sector. These visits were warmly received by the leaders of these countries, and my discussions with them increased my understanding of the role of people in the South in working towards building balanced growth in the world and a lasting peace for humanity that did not feature walls – physical or metaphorical – between nations.

It seemed to me that these walls and barriers were constantly being built and their height increased with every step the South took towards reducing the distance between it and the North. As Isaac Newton was wont to say during his time 300 years ago: *"We build too many walls and not enough bridges."* But I was always inclined to Chancellor Willy Brandt's position of optimism when he observed: "In the history of calamities that befall humanity, demolished bridges are inevitably rebuilt," adding: "The bridges between the North and the South have not collapsed yet." Fortunately so.

The late French president, François Mitterrand identified this relationship between the North and South in the preface of a reference book he wrote about Willy Brandt, considering North/South relations to be "severely imbalanced, to the degree that thirst for dignity carries in its folds an internal rage which may lead it to explode unexpectedly". He could have been predicting events which would take place later, catalysed by the anger of the Tunisian streets and followed by the Arab streets exploding in their cries for freedom and national dignity amongst the events of the Arab Spring. Mitterrand adds that there are "increasing ties that pull the economies of the world together, as well as cultural influences that meander from culture to culture and distances that are increasingly shrinking so that nations become neighbours, one to another, regardless of their geographical location. That is why humanity today, more than ever before, is equally responsible for its own destiny and free to make its own choice as to whether to move in the right direction or to remain ossified."

Humanity has gone through many trials which have put the ideals championed by the countries of the North to the test, perhaps the most prominent of these being COVID-19, where the Northern nations realised that they were facing the spectre of this pandemic alone; and that their proclaimed virtue of solidarity was baseless, for each nation underwent the tribulations of facing the pandemic without support of its neighbours and allies. This was a significant lesson in how quickly these principles were shed and cast aside in real life.

It therefore behoves us to ask: Did countries combat the pandemic in a genuine spirit of humanitarian solidarity, or was each nation content to shut its borders and protect its citizens without care for others? The fact is that when we still believed the novel coronavirus could be eradicated, it would have been necessary for all nations on earth to co-ordinate resources and demonstrate global solidarity, because the virus knows no colour, no race and no culture. Its spread could not be restricted by closing borders; and no wall could stop it whether travelling from North to South or vice-versa. Yet even then, we did not take heed and combine our efforts to work on a truly global scale. Instead, each country plotted its own course, whether to the detriment of others or not.

Doubtless, a grave and conspicuous environmental injustice currently exists, the roots of which may be traced back to the countries of the North. Its wealth and burgeoning capitalism could only have come about as a result of its careless use of the environment. Most of the pollution that causes our planet to suffer emanates from the industrialised countries of the North in conjunction with China, which has led to the countries of the South footing the bill for pollution and climate change in terms of their citizens' health and countries' economies. We witness extended droughts in large areas of Africa and Asia as a direct result of climate change caused by countries of the North, just as we see wildfires and floods that extinguish lives, lay waste to crops and decimate livestock. Instead of offering reasonable compensation for these losses and striving to avoid or minimise them in the future, we see the countries of the North spend extortionate sums of money on weapons. As I mentioned previously to the United Nations representative in UNESCO when he was questioning me during my candidacy for Director General, the price of one single rocket launched by American carriers would easily solve UNESCO's budget deficit, which in turn would serve science, education and culture for all the countries of the world. From another perspective, it's clear that the needs of the countries of the South in the field of education, for example, are simple needs that do not require huge amounts of funding. That was the reason I dedicated part of my electoral programme to what I called "micro-projects in education". The intention was to finance projects whose costs did not exceed $20,000 yet would still yield tangible results, such as the building of a school or the payment of teachers' salaries and other such practical expenditures that palpably facilitate the spread of education in the countries of the South.

Awareness of the imminent danger posed by pollution and recognising its all-pervasive nature, which has no respect for geopolitical borders forces the environmental question to become a global dilemma par excellence. This danger is transposed onto the fierce face of the countries of the North, where capitalism cares more about its own quick profit than it does about human health. Industry and governments are well aware of the existence of clean energy sources that do not pollute the environment but insist on using non-renewable sources that lead to widespread pollution.

Environmental advocates, therefore, talk about managing the climate issue globally and about an international community which has a vested interest in defending the environment as communal property. An international community that is forced, in the face of the imminent dangers of fires, floods, epidemics and other disasters resulting from climate change, to abandon its selfish, narrow-minded nationalism and backwards dichotomous perception of a bifurcated world, split between North and South. And when global civil society refers to environmental justice, this actually means demanding that the countries of the North – that is, the major polluters – reduce their greenhouse gas emissions in order to limit the rise in global temperatures to 1.5 degrees Celsius whilst simultaneously financing the means and methods that will mitigate their negative effects on the countries of the South, which are the ones that bear the worst consequences of climate change without actually being responsible for it.

The Chapter of Grievances

Chancellor Willy Brandt said: "Never forget, he who commits a grievance opens the door to other grievances."

I share his opinion. I have been invited to listen to speeches on universal rights many times, all of which have remained as mere ink on paper – words that do not leave the page or manifest in real life. It angered and frustrated me that in the end, only the wealthy countries of the North would benefit from these flowery phrases. I know, full well, that they invented a cosmetic phrase to describe the reality of the contempt felt by countries of the North towards countries of the South: "Realpolitik". A term, pronounced in German - its original language - in order to beautify ugliness with a linguistic veneer which refers to the politics of reality and a shift away from dreams and wishful thinking. It is good to be realistic, but to what purpose? Is the intention to disseminate despair, frustration and depression, and to remain content with misery and injustice?

I am not a proponent of the theory that labels man as a wolf towards their fellow humans. It would be more accurate to say that there are wolves who roam amongst men and agitate for racial superiority and have delusions that some civilisations are superior to others. At the end of the 19th century, some voices rose to defend colonialism; arguing that the countries of the North – specifically the West – would bring civilisation to the countries of the South. The West may have brought technical progress, but it cannot claim to have spread civilisation, for each culture has its own specific civilisation. An example not limited to Arab Muslims is their previous and stable civilization in human history. Furthermore, a lack of insight and true perception caused the colonialist mentality to spread around the world on the basis of ridiculous, flimsy justifications. In 1885, a heated debate took place in the French parliament which consisted of a stand-off between politicians who were against colonialist philosophies and those who supported them. Jules Ferry was a fierce defender of colonialism, whereas Georges Clemenceau opposed it vehemently.

In Georges Clemenceau's famous speech to the parliament, he answered Jules Ferry thus: "From an economic perspective, the matter appears to be quite simple for Monsieur Ferry, who has an oven-ready recipe – 'Do you want markets for your products? That is enough to establish colonies. There will be new consumers who have needs and who have not previously purchased from your markets. And by communicating with your civilisation, they will develop those needs. Establish commercial relations with them and try to create ties by way of treaties that will be carried out'. This is the theory of colonial outputs, which claims that in order to create products, you need to wage wars in the farthest corners of the world, and when you spend hundreds of millions and kill thousands of French people in order to arrive at this result, you will achieve what you want in direct proportion to the amount of dead people and as many millions as you have spent, in addition to other expenses and overheads. The products and outputs will all be… cul de sacs. Monsieur Ferry claims that superior races have legitimate rights over the inferior races, and this right is somehow simultaneously transformed into 'a duty to civilise'. These are Monsieur Ferry's statements and we witness the French government weaponizing its right over these inferior races, for it goes forth to wage wars against them and forcibly transforms them in order for these races to benefit from the advantages of civilisation. In summary, therefore, they entrench the theory of superior and inferior races. For my part, I do not follow this futile nonsense, especially since I heard German scientists 'prove scientifically' that France must be defeated in the Franco-German war because the French belong to a race that is inferior to the German race. And I confess that since then, I think twice before referring to a person or a civilisation and uttering the phrase: '…an inferior people, or an inferior civilisation'."

Despite all this, Clemenceau's enlightened stance did not prevent Jules Ferry's supporters and followers from establishing settlements and massacring millions of human beings. Will humanity not take heed?

Is it not time to establish peaceful relations between the North and South? Does the North not yet feel the enormity of its surfeit harvest from the countries of the South? The time has come to correct this trajectory and, for consciences active in the struggle towards justice and the march to narrow the chasm between the wealthy North and miserable South, the time is now.

Chapter Three
"All the rivers flow into the sea, yet the sea is not full."
Chinese proverb

Has Orientalism Really Disappeared?

The researcher doesn't need much time or effort to ascertain that human history consists of a consecutive series of eras, each dominated by a specific culture, geographic space, nation or people. This is an epic that stretches throughout the length of consecutive civilisations, interspersed with periods of glory, prosperity and greatness, or the converse – failure, poverty and weakness.

This discrepancy between nations is made evident in the cycle of civilisations. Although their differences do not preclude their participation in human civilisation, the criteria deciding these disparities have become biased as a result of Eurocentric approaches, in which Europe presents itself as the ideal model and the ideal standard by which civilisations can be measured. The term 'civilised nations' has been used to justify this Eurocentrism which has morphed into imperialism. Had it not been for the struggle of colonised peoples, the West would not had stopped calling them 'barbarians' and 'savages', nor would it have realised – after a siesta spanning several centuries – that human civilisation is not a Western creation.

Our cultural discourse has long suffered from Orientalism and its evil, which nobody can deny, in addition to its distortion of the image of Arabs and Muslims. Despite my appreciation for French philosophy, and specifically the Age of Enlightenment, I still remember what shocked me when I leafed through the pages of the philosopher Montesquieu's book – a proponent of the theory of the separation of powers. He refers to the 'tyranny of Islam' and its incompatibility with the West in his two books, *The Spirit of the Law* and *Persian Letters*. Thus, such ideas paved the way for colonialism whilst also granting it intellectual and psychological legitimacy.

The colonial era has ended, but Orientalism remains ingrained in our lives and flows through the veins of the Western world's relations with the Arab world. The West has now come to think of Arabs and the wider East via the legacy of Orientalism, and sees nothing but weak, helpless peoples. This is what Edward Said noted in his renowned book on Orientalism, where he acknowledges its presence as an epistemological methodology that reflects Western perceptions based on a world view that holds the Orient to be inferior in relation to the Occident. According to Said, the West was able to contain the Orient and ossify it into a limited frame. He said: "The Orient will appear to be a closed field or a stage merely appended to Europe, rather than an unlimited extension outwith the familiar European world." [1]

A theatre populated by myths of the Sphinx, Cleopatra, the Garden of Eden and others. It is well known that the Orientalists' reading of Arab literature alongside their preconceptions of its inferiority helped perpetuate their stance vis-à-vis the Orient. Not to mention that for decades, Westerners believed that the Orient

---

1 Edward Said, Orientalism – Western Conceptions of the Orient, tr. Muhammad Enany. Ru'yah Publishers, first edition, 2006, p129.

was merely a night from the *Thousand and One Nights* – incapable of being anything more than a figment of literary imagination.

Following his meticulous studies, Edward Said confirmed this decisive definition of Orientalism as: "A Western method of dominating the East, causing it to be built up and possessing full sovereignty over it."[1] He expresses his fear of a far more dangerous phenomenon, namely, the encroachment of Orientalism into Arab thought, by saying: "However, Orientalism continues to thrive in many forms, despite its many failures, its pitiful lack of logic, its thinly-veiled racism and its paper-thin intellectual framework. Indeed, there is much cause for concern that its influence has spread to the East itself."[2]

The truth of the matter is that many elites who hail from the Arab world were not spared the ravages of Orientalism, neither were the concepts of "modernisation" and "enlightenment" spared from its clutches. Hence, our reading of Arab-Islamic heritage was also not spared from the Orientalist perspective, its tools of description, analysis and conclusion, just as any criticism of heritage continues to face conservative fears regarding the infiltration of Orientalism. Abdulrahman Badawi eloquently describes this: "Perhaps the power of Orientalism continues to exist until now, in the absence of the total collapse of Arab-Islamic heritage, the latter being a haunted castle, despite various efforts to enlighten it which are met with rejection from time to time. Critique of heritage is not a light matter – achieving a break with it cannot begin without systematically mastering it, highlighting and being aware of its limits, obstacles and its reasonable and unreasonable aspects."[3]

---

1 Edward Said, Orientalism – Power and Knowledge, tr. Kamal Abu Deeb, Arab Foundation for Research, Beirut, 2005, p39.
2 Op.cit.
3 Abdul Rahman Badawi in an interview with Hamish Bensalem, Al-Wihda Magazine, Number 17, volume 2 February 1986, page 160.

It should not be forgotten that Orientalism painted its own image of Islam and the Orient through the prism of its knowledge of heritage and its treasures. This reality cannot be corrected, except by a re-examination of source heritage material on the one hand, and an evaluation of the Orientalist experience on the other, without omitting the historical role played by the Orientalist themselves.

The favours paid to Arabic and Islamic studies by Orientalism are substantial, and none but the ignorant will deny this. During my life as a diplomat, I encountered many Orientalists who held a candle for Arab-Islamic heritage, cherishing it with respect and appreciation; some of them contributing to the discovery of valuable heritage books and struggling greatly with their editing. That is why it is impossible to tar all Orientalists with the same brush. No matter how much the different schools of Orientalist thought disagree with one another, they have all contributed towards sparking debate about Arab culture and civilisational history and energised inert scholars.

In order for us to view Orientalism objectively and without prejudice, it is more fitting that we should make use of the huge amount of Oriental studies, whether by accepting, critiquing or evaluating them. This is because our Arab culture will not develop in a vacuum or in isolation, devoid of dynamic dialogue with the perceptions and assumptions that others hold of us and our heritage. Here, I share the thinker Fouad Zakaria's opinion when he said: "Orientalism is not a pure, unsullied discipline, but a greater danger lies in us denying our faults simply because others point them out with ulterior motives. Our role, culturally, lies in grabbing the bull of backwardness by the horns and critiquing ourselves before criticising the image that others create about us, even though this image is only intended to distort." [1]

---

1 Fouad Zakaria, A Critique of Orientalism and the Crisis of Contemporary Arab Culture, Hindawi Foundation for publishing and translation, UK, p 71

If the Western Orientalist challenged Arab and Islamic thought by way of imposing their own approaches, then the methods used did not deviate from Eurocentrism or from referring to one single epistemological and civilisational model. How Arab & Islamic philosophy suffered as a result of systematic Western projections, not to mention Muhammad Abid Al Jabri's warning: "This is how the Orientalist, owner of this historic approach, perceives the entirety of Islamic philosophy, not as a part of or as an element of the general Arab-Islamic cultural entity, but by describing it as a perverted or distorted extension of Greek philosophy."[1]

Based on this diagnosis of Orientalism, I draw closer to the interaction between civilisations and observe how we Arabs deal with the discourse of the Other, whilst the Western Other remains unmoving in their self-perceived lofty position. Thus, our civilisation has been oppressed many times through the ages and has suffered Orientalist injustice since the 19th century. Our civilisation continues to suffer till this very day, but in different ways.

Orientalist thought appropriated our cultural history, believing that a linear history that builds up to a "glorious climax" is a monopoly of the West alone, and that Arab Muslims' efforts over the centuries are only destined for museums. By this means, the West continues to both control and model means of progress, while we remain trailing in backwardness and retardation!

Slogans on Progress – Two Sides of the Coin

I have always thought about factors that cause slogans to become merely fleeting words, followed by nothing more than conflicting policies, in various cultural contexts. For example, the French Revolution that broke out in 1789 raising the slogan "Liberté,

---

1 Muhammad 'Abid Al-Jabbari, Heritage and Modernity: Studies and Dialogue, The Arab Centre for Culture, Morocco, first edition, 1991, p.28

égalité, fraternité" was followed by Napoleon's campaign against Egypt less than 10 years later. Therefore, the prudent scholar should neither surrender to nor be misled by these slick slogans long feted by the West in the name of "progress", for the West has deliberately ignored the fact that the peoples who experienced the horrors of colonialism were, in the past, creators of civilisation. However, their contributions to and role in 'progress' – contributions which the West has attempted to erase – have survived nonetheless.

The key contention rests in the coupling of the two concepts 'civilisation' and 'progress'. The criteria by which civilisation is measured becomes reliant on the extent to which any one nation possesses specific manifestations of superiority that cause it to colonise others and plunder their goods and resources. This superiority subsumes everything connected with moral and religious infrastructures and life itself, until civilisation becomes, in the words of Mu'taz Abu Qasim, "a place that permits the demeaning of others and describes them as primitive savages or half-savages." Regardless of how sophisticated or not a nation becomes, it will never be acknowledged or accepted as such unless it conforms to Western-centric norms. Subordination is a foregone conclusion whether sooner – in which case you are feted – or later, in which case you are humiliated. [1]

This trend towards classifying nations as savage or civilised is explained by the West's insistence on its own definitions when addressing the issue of 'progress', tying itself inextricably to two essential concepts, 'development' and 'change' following Darwinian philosophy and research. This frame of reference robs the term 'progress' from any ethical or moral aspect, given that it is a socio-historical concept intrinsically linked to values, as the philosopher Fahmy Jada'an insisted when considering the "definition of

---

1 Charles Seignobos, History of Ancient Civilisation, tr. Muhammad Kurdi 'Ali, edited and presented by Mu'taz Abu Qasim, Al-Ahliyya Publishing, first edition, 2018, p 6

progress to be primarily a normative moral concept"[1]. He ruled that this concept could not possibly have stemmed from the scientific industrial revolution nor from Darwinian philosophy, but that its indications and manifestations may be traced back to civilisations with a more ancient history. He pointed to the fact that the difference between the ancient and the contemporary understanding of progress is that for ancient civilizations, progress was "metaphysical in nature, or an emotion reflecting human's wishes, hope and desire in attaining a particular(ly desirable) stage that is better than the preceding stage or stages. As for modern times, they have caused this concept to become a realistic, tangible one and not merely a utopian reflection of idealistic hopes and dreams alongside their self-appropriation of the ability to justify the concept, believing in its veracity in the annals of history and throughout mankind's movement and activities".[2]

Perhaps the tragedy which befell peoples throughout the decades of modern empires was manifested in the weaponization of the concepts of progress or civilisation into a pretext for colonisation and extermination. I read Munir Al-Akash's book, "America and Genocides", and felt sorrow and resentment. I did not expect that this pretext would permit the extermination of peoples in cold blood. I was overcome by pictures of Native Americans undergoing the most horrific forms of ethnic cleansing known to humanity, as what is termed "The New World" was emptied of its original inhabitants. The West concealed this, claiming that what had taken place was a result of natural causes or epidemics that wiped out more than 400 nations or tribes that were resident in North America.

The Native Americans were no more than a single link in a long chain that started in Ireland and demonstrated the colonialist

---

1   Fahmy Jada'an, The Principles of Progress in contemporary Muslim intellectuals' thought, Dar Al-Shuruq, third edition, 1988, p 19
2   Op. cit.

mentality that controlled the English – the "Divine Right to Rule" complex – as well as their belief in their own racial superiority, which was enforced by their behaviour and firearms. This complex took possession of their minds and their morals, subsequently colonising them with a complete infrastructure of delirious psychosis leading to self-deification. It is this which deluded them into believing that they have the right to apportion life and death to everyone but them; and that they are also free from any human or legal obligations to the nations which they have colonialised, considering that they are nothing but inferior races. In fact, they are nothing more than savage creatures that do not belong to the human race.[1]

This – the West – is the Pinnacle of Civilisation!

Can a sane person ever accept the erasure of centuries of historical facts, events and realities merely because they are not consistent with a particular culture's perspective, or because a certain culture openly agitates for the obliteration of all material and intangible features of another? Indeed, all human gains and achievements to this present day are nothing more than the culmination of various civilisations' accomplishments in all fields of knowledge. However, since the start of the industrial age, Western thinkers took to disseminating the belief that the West was the pinnacle of civilisation and this view remained prevalent until it was shaken by the rebellion of youth in France during May 1968, soon after the colonies gained independence. America and Europe then experienced revisionary events of their own which led them to correct these ideas, but they were revisions that pained the narcissism of a self-proclaimed uniquely civilised role.

---

1   Munir Al-'Aksh America and her Genocides, AlReys Publishing House, first edition, 2002, p57-58

Let us remind the West that Western computers use algorithms invented by Al-Khwarizmi in the Middle Ages, and that the whole world uses scientific research principles that were laid down by Ibn Al-Haytham, just as we all use paper invented by the Chinese and so on. If every single human civilisation decided to isolate itself and be satisfied with its own inventions and discoveries, to the exclusion of those of other civilisations, we would never have reached this stage of technological advancement. The writer Tahar Ben Jelloun portrays a similar scenario brilliantly and sarcastically in order to show all level-minded people what the consequences might be should each civilisation claim its own culture only and reclaim it, returning esoterically to its own lands. The Moroccan author imagined the exodus of Arabs from France, and the consternation that this would cause in an article published in the columns of *Le Monde Diplomatique* [The World of Diplomacy] newspaper titled "Le dernier immigré – The Last Migrant". [1]

He wrote: "This morning, the final Arab immigrant – a Berber in fact – departed, leaving French soil. The First Minister and the Minister of the Interior also travelled in order to attend this departure and to convey France's debt of gratitude to Mr Muhammad Lemghri. Muhammad was neither moved nor angry, he was simply happy with the prospect of the final return to his country of origin. He received a few gifts in the form of a small camel-shaped model and a small flag decorated in blue, white and red on one side and with a green star on the other. He was waving the flag desultorily in front of the paparazzi and television cameras, who insisted that he smile for them. He burst out laughing and put the duplicitous flag into the pocket of his old coat."

---

1   The original French article appears in Le Monde Diplomatique, in August 2006 on the paper's website https://www.monde-diplomatique.fr/2006/08/BEN_JELLOUN/13757

Using the medium of black humour, Ben Jelloun describes the consequences of the migrant's departure as France breathes a sigh of relief after he packs his bags, drawing a century of innumerable uncontrollable problems to a close – the problems of immigrants' customs and traditions, problems of racism and the myth of the slogan of integration. He also portrays the suffering of the far-right as a result of this departure, as right-wing extremism loses its trump card. This loss explains the raised voices during protests calling: "Bring back our Arabs, whom we love unconditionally, without borders!" and "France isn't the same – she misses her Arab family grocery!" For Arabs are like the fuel in the furnace of hatred. Sardonically, Ben Jelloun uncovers the fate of the French language when it loses dozens of borrowed words from the Arab immigrants' records, causing news articles to be incomplete and discourse to become filled with gaps. So it is that the immigrants' exodus from France threatens the French language into which Arabic words have seeped. In this somewhat fantastical narrative, Ben Jelloun describes how the linguists become nonplussed by this state of affairs and how renowned French dictionaries such as *Grand Larousse, Grand Robert* and *Hachette-Oxford* tumble from the bookshelves of a library. How, when a librarian opens one of the dictionaries, she notices the empty white pages and watches in a state of suspended disbelief as the letters and words tumble to the ground! Panic spreads until it reaches the French scientific authorities, and a meeting is arranged to discuss the outcome of this situation. The linguist Alain Rey now intervenes to try to explain the horrific extent of this catastrophe when the French language is stripped bare of Arabic words. Here, Ben Jelloun speaks from the impartial French intellectual's perspective, using Rey's voice to defend the impossibility of divesting *Molière's* language of Arabic words: "There are hundreds of words that have entered our language without a visa or border control. Without these words, science would have been sick, there would have been no mathematics without Arabs, no numbers, no algebra and no algorithms. These words naturally entered the French language and enriched it until they have become, quite simply, indispensable. We have imported them, or more accurately, borrowed them because we needed them and nobody ever imagined that they would, one day, expel them or that they would desert us, endangering France's psychological balance!"

The situation deteriorates to the extent that the President of the French Republic intervenes, delivering a speech during the principal news broadcast castigating the idea of deporting Arabs from France and displacing them. In a caricature-like scene, Ben Jelloum combines his veiled criticism of French immigration policies and his reference to France's inability to rid herself of Arabs because they had become an intrinsic component of her cultural identity! The President speaks thus:

> "*Frenchwomen, Frenchmen – dear French citizens:*
> *Assalamu 'alaykum!*
> *Yes, you heard correctly! Assalamu 'alaykum means good evening in Arabic, or to be precise: May peace be upon you.*
> *Ladies and gentlemen – mesdames et messieurs !*
> *I will not keep you long – Je serai bref.*
> *France has not only made a mistake, it has committed a great injustice! (he repeats in Arabic: A great injustice!).*
> *After the 11th of September 2001, some people said: "We are all Americans!" Today, I proclaim: "We are all Arabs!"*
> *We are all Arabs! We are all immigrants!*
> *By behaving in this manner, we have offended their dignity, we have lost ourselves and our own dignity. (He repeats in Arabic: our own dignity).*
> *I know I will not be re-elected. It does not matter. I will not nominate myself again. I honour the Arabic language and culture in the hope that there will be some who might accept to return to France so that they may set her back on her feet.*
> *Assalamu 'alaykum! Long live France! Long live the Arab Maghreb!"*

When Europe Loses her Memory

Al Tahar Ben Jalloun entrusted Alain Rey, the French linguist and editor-in-chief of the renowned *Petit Robert* dictionary, with the starring protagonist's role in order to correct the preconceived prejudices in the play that he imagined. Rey died on November the 28th, 2020 and a state funeral was held in honour of his contributions to the French language.

In truth, there are a large number of fair-minded intellectuals who do not accept racism and prejudice based on preconceived ideas that spread hatred and discord between nations. They reject the ideas exploited by the extreme right in order to whip up popular opinion and gain votes all over the world, such as thinkers like Todorov who began his life story with an intense fascination over West leading to his initial support of the American war on Vietnam and ending in a complete rejection of American hegemony over the world, in addition to a forensic dissection of Europe beginning with questioning the age of enlightenment and concluding with a condemnation of European actions based on the age of enlightenment that legitimised colonialism.

Anti-migrant ideology continued, as did attempts to kill off positive memories in order that Europeans may deny the roots of their Renaissance firstly; and secondly, the participation of any other than them in their own civilization. It is clear that Huntington's ideas did not emanate from a vacuum, rather they are born of the historical context in which the West denies the virtue of other civilizations. That is why he was emboldened to state: "The Western culture is challenged by various societies. One of these challenges comes from migrants of other civilizations who refused to become assimilated; and continue to nurture connections to, as well as values and traditions of their own society. This phenomenon is most evident amongst Muslims in Europe." [1]

Western culture deliberately forgot the ills that afflicted it at a time when the Arab Islamic civilisation was at its peak; and ignored the darkness that was its lived experience during the Middle Ages, whilst a single European patch of culture managed to escape from this darkness thanks to the Arab Muslims.

We wonder, is it possible to understand Spain, for example, without Arab culture? Is it possible to deny that the unusual, precise crafts that Spain is proud of — the administrative organisation, the military, navigation, medicine and economics are all derived from the Arabic language and its civilisation?

The attempt to amputate memory and seal it off continues to this day in Spain, although the Arab Islamic presence in Andalusia and its legacy of over eight centuries cannot be forgotten, nor can the thousands of words derived from the Arabic language be overlooked. Anyone who believes that it is possible for the Spanish to speak about Spanish identity without the Arab Islamic cultural component is deluding themselves.

The persecution of Arab Muslims after the Fall of Granada was manifold, for not only did it include physical persecution, torture, killing, displacement and exile, but it also involved outlawing Arab dress and forbade speaking in Arabic. Books of all genres were seized, confiscated or stolen either by burning them, blurring their owners' identity, or smuggling them to Europe. Literary theft in the Middle Ages was considered to be a means by which the contributions that Arabs made to knowledge and science could be erased. As Fuat Sezgin, mathematician, historian and professor emeritus in the history of natural sciences at Goethe University in Frankfurt, said: "In the Italian city of Salerno, 25 volumes were translated into Latin with no mention of their original authors.

---

1 Samuel Huntingdon, Op. cit. p508

This was an entirely normal approach in Europe during the Middle Ages. In the 20th century, we discovered that these books were written by Arab scholars, and that they were translated after being stolen, without any reference whatsoever being made to their original authors, whether directly or indirectly."

The Middle Ages witnessed the violence of the Inquisition and the spread of hostility towards knowledge in the name of religious tutelage over humanity's conscience. Neither the Arab Muslims in Andalusia nor the European scholars, philosophers and writers themselves were spared this oppression. They were victims of the Christian Church's intolerance and fanaticism that stooped as low as to issue its infamous list of prohibited books[1] and forbid its followers from reading them. It mobilised guards and soldiers to burn them wherever they were found. Naturally, the Noble Qur'an was at the top of the list which also included the works of hundreds of European authors. The Church continued to update this list, diligently adding new authors, both men and women to this repository of forbidden knowledge until 1968.

In his novel *The Name of the Rose*, the Italian philosopher and author Umberto Eco revealed the extent to which the Church deliberately obstructed science and prevented the acquisition of knowledge by portraying knowledge as the great metaphor for death, actively disseminating the idea that every soul yearning to discover the knowledge contained in books of philosophy and enlightenment will be doomed to die. In a very real sense, knowledge is death, for the plot of the novel revolves around the Franciscan investigator Guillermo Baskerville's attempts to discover

---

[1] The original list of prohibited books and their titles in Latin: Index Librorum Prohibitorum, is a list that the Christian Church stove to keep updated and includes hundreds of works by authors, philosophers, writer, intellectuals, natural scientist of all persuasions who the Church forbade the reading or perusal of. It did not stop updating this list until the 1960s.

who is lacing the pages of a book with deadly poison, causing whoever turns the pages to die.

It is every society's right to deal with its own collective memory in the manner it deems appropriate, but it would be unfair to create a montage out of this memory that excises the role of the Other in building their own civilisational entity. I am well aware of the impossibility of preserving the past in its pure form, exactly as it occurred historically. When we remember the past, we do not remember it in the way it happened. What remains is what the collective memory is capable of preserving depending on fluctuating historical circumstances and according to new political and cultural frameworks, for we always undertake to [re]build the past according to the ties that bind us together within a historical framework governed by constant change.

Patches of successive disappointments begin to appear in the face of deepening holes in memory, as the arrogance of material progress that is the West's lived experience cannot erase other civilisations' contributions to this self-same progress from human memory. If the West were to be divided between two regions – Europe and North America, then "old" Europe seems to be a source of many disappointments for both Western and Arab intellectuals alike. I mirror Amin Maalouf's grief as he exposes his "wounds" in his book *The Drowning of Civilisations* when he says: "I do not wish to belittle the many forms of enormous progress that Europeans have made since the end of the Second World War; and I welcome these with all my heart. Despite this, I cannot deny that today I feel somewhat disappointed. I expected something different from my adopted continent – to provide humanity with a compass with which to avoid fragmentation and obsolescence, to prevent it from shattering into tribes, associations, factions and clans."[1]

---

1   Amin Ma'alouf, Drowned Civilisations, Dar Al-Farabi, first edition 2019 p265

Do I, in turn, feel this disappointment? I spent decades working in the fields of culture and diplomacy, full of hope and optimism despite the bitter reality of Western centralism, the dissipation of the ideal image of European enlightenment, the broken promises and the failure of European philosophies when it comes to simple litmus tests, including that of UNESCO elections. Despite all this, I still pin hope on a European and American intellectual elite who believe in self-criticism and have a certain degree of respect and reverence for the human dimension of different civilisations.

I am certain that what is happening in the West is not specific or limited to centralised thought dressed in Western ideas only. We, in our own civilisations, have also suffered from similar tumours that impeded the movement of a healthy body of civilisation and strived to curb creativity in many intellectual arenas. There is no doubt that many cultures have created "thought-gaolers" who suppress any intellectual activity or literary production that is not in agreement with prevailing thought. In Andalusia, Muslim extremists burned valuable books including the works of the Andalusian philosopher Ibn Rushd. In fact, the researcher Lucien X. Polastron devoted an entire publication, entitled *Books on Fire: The Destruction of Libraries throughout History,* to this issue, in which he chronicles the burning of intellectual works throughout the ages and in many different places and human civilisations. This is because the voices that gatekeep prevalent mainstream narrative and call for the marginalisation of enlightened thought are not monolithic. Rather, they hail from many diverse races, yet their hearts are all united against enlightenment!

In the face of this tendency towards intolerance and the denial of the role played by Arab Muslims in human civilisation, a few sincere and objective voices emerge to acknowledge this role. However, I always wonder whether these voices genuinely emanate from within the core of Eurocentric culture, or merely from the periphery.

Objective works of Western writers no longer shake this entrenched centralism because it is incapable of permeating any official cultural decision-making, nor have any major impact on any political decision affecting Western cultures. Let us turn, for example, to the German orientalist Sigrid Hunke as a prime example. In her book *The Arab Sun shines on the West*, she clearly describes this prism of superiority that Western cultures espouse when interacting with Arab Islamic civilisations. She says: "It seems to me that the time has come to speak of a people who have strongly influenced the course of global events, to whom the West is indebted; just as humanity as a whole is considerably indebted. Despite this, a person who reads through a hundred history books will find no mention of this people's name in 98 of them."[1]

This is why only an ignoramus would deny the contributions made by Arab Islamic civilisations that enriched human thought generally, in all material and intellectual aspects including systems of governance, science, knowledge, arts and aesthetics as I will demonstrate.

Arabian Lights

In his last interview, Jean-Baptiste Brenet, philosopher and professor of Arabic philosophy at the University of Paris, praised the efforts of the early Arab philosophers and thinkers,[2] debunking the prevalent narrative in the West that Arabs were merely conduits of knowledge who conveyed Greek philosophy. In his opinion, a conduit is one who conveys something with a great deal of

---

[1] Sigrid Hunke The Arab's sun shines over the West, taken from the original German by Farouq Baydoun, Kamal Dessouqui, see Maroun Isa Alkhouri, Dar Al-Jil, eighth edition, 1993, p 11

[2] See the interview transcript published in "La Philosophie Arabe ne s'est pas fait malgre elle, par hazard et passivement" on French Philosophy's website: www.philomag.com, accessed 14/10/2021

objectivity and without adding any meaningful contribution, personal creativity or invention. However, the early Arabs' efforts did not stop at knowledge transfer, for in addition to the virtuous role played by Arab thought in connecting Westerners to their roots in Greek philosophy they were also able to gather up all the scattered manuscripts on philosophy and care for them in their dilapidated state. Some were familiar with Syriac, so undertook to unearth, research and edit manuscripts from the Syriac language for presentation in an acceptable format to the West. These were then translated from Arabic into Latin, including the favour Al-Kindi performed in the ninth century CE when he translated Aristotle's *Theology*, which mainly consists of a creative rewriting of Plato's writings. Brenet considers the ancient Arab philosophers to be more than mere recipients of philosophical knowledge, but creative innovators who contributed to this corpus by selectively choosing to keep what was appropriate to their identity and thought and enriching these aforementioned Greek sources with their own commentaries. Even Aristotle, who was discovered by Latinophiles in the 12th century, was imbued with Arab heritage and born afresh from another womb to disseminate the original Greek logos in an innovative new form.

This equity was not confined to a few contemporary thinkers but is evident in the many works of historians and travellers, who did not only look to the legacies left by the Arab-Islamic civilisation, but also experienced Arab life and came to realise the real influence that the Arabs had on human civilisation, particularly in the West. I remember Gustav Le Bon's interesting book in which he said: "The more deeply we study Arab civilisation, their scientific books, their inventions and their arts, the more new facts and expansive horizons appear to us; and the more speedily we see that the Arabs should be credited for the knowledge that the Medieval world had of the science of the ancients. Also, that for five whole centuries, the universities of the West had no scientific resource available to them other than these books; and that they were the ones who civilised Europe materially, morally and mentally. History has never witnessed a nation that has produced what they have produced in such a short time span. They were unparalleled in the field of artistic creativity and innovation."[1]

Amongst the works of Orientalists that I have read, I found Spanish Orientalism to be fairer than others vis-à-vis Arab-Islamic contributions. I wondered about the reasons for this and sensed a pure scientific spirit in the works of Spanish Orientalists, to the extent that I believe that Arab blood flowed through their veins. My readings include the work of the Orientalist Juan Vernet, founder of the Barcelona School of Historians of Medieval Science and in my opinion the subject of Arab civilisation is more easily accessible to Spanish Orientalists due to the fact that it was present in Spain. Despite the rifts that occurred when the Muslims were expelled and exiled, it is impossible to extricate itself from their shared history, the effects of which manifest themselves right up to the present day – not only in terms of architecture, but in the realms of customs, societal practices and traditions.

Arab Civilisation and the System of State Governance

There is no doubt that Arab and Muslim scholars benefited greatly from the Greek, Roman and Persian civilisations and that they excelled in translating the most valuable and prominent of books. However, this benefit was not one-sided nor was it limited to simply appropriating and copying, but was characterised by creativity and enhancement, so they contributed the essential building blocks and

---

1   Gustav Le Bon "Arab Civilisation" tr. Adil Zeitreh, Hindawi Foundation, published 2013, p 30

paved the way for science, lighting the torch to whose light the West is indebted.

Ibn Al-Muqaffa' was the first to write boldly on the issue of governance, an acceptable modern translation of what he briefly refers to in his writings as "Sultanic" or "Royal Ideology". This has had a pervasive and marked influence on Arab Islamic historical discourse, leaving behind a powerful legacy for all civilisations. Motivated by our awareness of inter-civilisational dynamics and a desire to move away from centralised discourse, we would like to point out that Arab civilisation has benefited enormously from other civilisations over the ages in building a unique perception of institutions that form a ruling system, including the Persian civilisation. This is because we believe that the application of anti-centralist discourse to any civilisation helps us present the Arab Islamic civilisation as one of the civilisations that influenced others and was influenced itself, without claiming absolute possession or civilisational precedence.

Ibn Al-Muqaffa' was preoccupied with Sultanic literature during the Abbasid era and employed his seminal books such as "al-Adab al-Saghir wal-Adab al-Kabir" and "Risalat al-Sahabah" to explain the system of governance both logically and ethically from a reformative perspective. He benefitted from Persian and Greek cultures to build an intellectual discourse around the specific relationship it had with the Sultan, as well as how to manage affairs of the state by infusing these cultural references into an Islamic worldview based on the principle of monotheism. Thus, Ibn Al-Muqaffa' embodied the image of an intellectual who is able to understand inter-civilisational dynamics in order to reform and improve political and social reality.

The Arabs continued to write copiously on the systems of government; and were not content with combining theoretical analysis with extrapolation of practice in society. Rather, they were deeply interested in different systems of government in various cultures, based on actual experiences of governance. Amongst the most famous works in this field is "Siraj al-Muluk" by Abu Bakr al-Tartushi, who lived in the fifth and sixth centuries of the Hijri calendar (11th and 12th centuries CE). He studied six nations comparatively: Arabs, Romans, Persians, Indian, Chinese and the Sindh [part of modern-day Pakistan) and wrote a volume consisting of 64 chapters in which he dealt with various fields relating to systems of government, including the art of governance and management of the affairs of subjects, the organisation of taxation and national defence, the characteristics of ministers and their positive qualities, the importance of seeking counsel and advice, and judiciously managing the affairs of cities and metropolises. Al-Tartushi also attached much importance to human nature and warned against the granting of ministerial powers to those of a sly, mean or crooked disposition, justifying his stance by saying: "A mean man - should he rise through the ranks - disowns his relatives, denies knowledge of his acquaintances, demeans nobility and is arrogant towards the virtuous." Al-Tartushi narrates an anecdote that occurred between Sulayman bin 'Abdul-Malik and 'Umar bin 'Abdul-Aziz: "When Sulayman bin 'Abdul-Malik wished to employ Al-Hajjaj Yazid bin Abi Muslim's scribe, 'Umar bin 'Abdul-Aziz said to him: "Oh Leader of the Faithful, I entreat you by Allah not to revive Al-Hajjaj's memory by employing [this man] as a scribe." He replied: "Oh Abu Hafs, I have not found him to betray either dinar or dirham." (i.e. I have not found him to be dishonest in financial dealings). 'Umar said: "I will find someone for you who is more honest in matters of the dinar and dirham." He asked: "And who would that be?" 'Umar replied: "Iblis (Satan), for he did not touch either dinar or dirham; and laid waste to this creation in its entirety."[1]

---

1   Abu Bakr Al-Tartushi, Siraj Al-Muluk, 1872, Egypt, p57

Also famous amongst political works is 'Abd al-Rahman al-Shaizari's "Manhaj Almasluk fi Siyasat AlMuluk" (Methodology Followed in the Policy of Kings), which was intended for the guidance of Salah al-Din al-Ayyubi. In the preface, its author describes it as: "...containing diverting anecdotes of wisdom, gems of literature, principles of politics and the fundamentals of managing subjects, knowledge regarding the kingdom's pillars and kingship, rules of management and the division of the spoils of war and booty amongst soldiers and what the army needs in terms of the rights of jihad. In this section I draw attention to both honourable character and reprehensible morals and allude to the virtue of consultation and urge that counsel should be sought, as well as how to resist and overcome enemies and military policy. In here, I have deposited the proverbs that have surfaced to the forefront of my mind as a result of their enactment before me or evidence that I have experienced leading me towards them, alongside rare snippets of news and quotations of poetry". [1] The author does not content himself with describing the instruments of government and good governance, but he also deals with problems that may befall him and studies the reasons behind the destruction of nations, directing his advice to Salah al-Din: "The reasons that lead to a king's downfall are three – the first of which emanates from the king; and that is his desires overwhelm his mind, allowing there to be no pleasure unless he consumes it and no comfort unless he assumes it. Secondly – ministers, as their envy necessitates a conflict of opinions. No (king) precedes them in reaching the truth, but they denounce and oppose it. Thirdly – from the army and dignitaries, which is abstaining from flogging and abandoning mutual advice in jihad." [2]

---

1   Abdulrahman bin Nasr Al-Shirazi, Al Nahj al Masluk fi Siyasat Al Muluk, Bahsoon Foundation for publishing and distribution, first edition, 1974 p158-159.
2   Op. cit. p557

No one can deny the virtue of the scholar Abd al-Rahman ibn Khaldun (1332 – 1406 CE) in laying the foundations of social, economic and political theories that apply to all human societies. Through his political and social experience, Ibn Khaldun was able to establish the "science of urbanisation"; and developed a holistic treatise on the state, in which he outlines the nature of the state and its institutions and discusses the principles upon which it is founded. He studies the reasons behind its creation, its development and its demise, paying particular attention to the laws that govern these stages. In his understanding of the concept of "'asabiyyah" – social cohesion – which he considers to be a key factor in the building of the state, Ibn Khaldun links the Bedouin and urban communities. His ideas have influenced global social thought and continue to do so, not to mention the fact that historian and philosopher Arnold Toynbee borrows heavily from Ibn Khaldun's ideas and uses them as a foundation on which he built his theory of "Challenge and Response". Toynbee divides societies into primitive and urban societies, believing that the origin of urban societies evolved from primitive societies, which he then categorises into six: Egyptian, Sumerian, Minoan, Mayan, Indian and Chinese. In Toynbee's thoughts regarding the stages of societal evolution, we find clear evidence of Ibn Khaldun's ideas, as Toynbee believes that all civilisations have experienced very similar stages of nascence, development and decline. Likewise, Ibn Khaldun acknowledges that states are similar in their stages of development and cycles; and that every state is built on the ruins of its predecessor.

In practice, the Arabs and Muslims generally relied on the principle of Shura – consultation or seeking counsel – and defined who they would consult by bestowing the title of "Ahl al-Shura" (or al-Hal wal-'Aqd), upon them, stipulating that they must be just, knowledgeable, righteous and possess wisdom and acuity. Imam Nawawi defines them thus: "Scholars, leaders and honourable people who may be conveniently gathered together".[1] It is worthy of note that the world was suffering under and drowning in the dominance of tyrannical and exclusionary ruling systems when Islam perfected the principle of Shura; and that Shura was a path to transforming the dominant narrative in empires and kingdoms that were contemporaneous to Muslim societies at the time.

For a similar form of governance, Europe would have to wait for Montesquieu to emerge to formulate a new political theory in his book *The Spirit of Laws*, in which he examined the political institutions of his time and came up with a new formula for government that remained open to the spirit of science and reason, contrary to the existing traditional and tyrannical formula. This took place after many centuries, during which Muslims had existed within the structure of the Shura system and had lived through different experiences based on this principle of governance.

Also prominent within the Arabs' intellectual output in the area of ruling systems is the issue of ministry – its organisation and importance. Here, the Arabs demonstrated wisdom and correctness in both theory and practice. In the matter of ministry, Ibn Khaldun says, alluding to the help and support offered by the ministers to the ruler: "It is the mother of Sultanic plans and the pinnacle of royal ranks, because its very name indicates unfettered assistance".[2] One of the finest ministers to have explored ruling systems and ministerial mechanisms is Nitham al-Mulk in his renowned work "Sayr al-Muluk", written for the Seljuk Sultan Malikshah bin Muhammad in order to guide him to successful methods of governance and rule as demonstrated by his predecessors. But the polymath Al-Mawardi preceded Nitham al-Mulk in theoretically dividing ministries into two categories – ministries of delegation

---

1   Abu Zakariyyah Muhiddin Yahya bin Sharaf Al-Nawwawi, "Al-Manhaj", p 12-77
2   Abdulrahman bin Khaldun, "Kitab Al-'Arab wa diwan al mubtada' wal khabar" Dar Al-Kitab Al-'Alami, 1995, vol 1, p236

and ministries of implementation. In the first, the ruler delegates the decision-making and organisation process to the minister, whereas a minister of implementation suffices himself with correctly carrying out the ruler's decisions and executing his orders as he would like them to be".[1] Then, the process of categorising ministries according to specialisation began in Muslim Arab Andalusian history. As Ibn Khaldun narrates: "As for the Umayyad State in Andalusia, they retained the original meaning associated with the title of minister at the beginning of the state. They then divided their portfolio into categories, appointing a minister to each. Thus, they appointed a minister for finances and accounting, a minister for postal services, a minister to investigate the affairs of claimants and petitioners, and a minister for the needy. A house was built for them to sit in and a desk prepared for them, at which each would carry out the Sultan's orders according to their own allocated remit. One of their number was appointed as a go-between, shuttling back and forth between the Khalifah and the group. His status was elevated due to his unfettered access to the Sultan at all times, so his desk was raised above the level of the others', and he was addressed by the title Al Hajib". [2]

It is clear that here Ibn Khaldun is referring to the prime minister in the same way he did at the start of his description of the ministers of finance, foreign affairs, justice and defence; and the house in which they meet as the Council of Ministers. Thus, it is clear that this ministerial organisation of the state began historically in Andalusia and spread from there all over the world. It is this system that Western countries later adopted as the structure of how they would govern their affairs. They also appointed ministers to specialisations according to their experience, skills set and knowledge under the prime minister's supervision of general

---

1   Abul Hassan 'Ali bin Muhannad Al Mawardi "Al-Ahkam Alsultaniyyah" Dar AlKitab Al'Alamiyyah, 2011 p 24-25

2   Op. cit. Ibn Khladun "Kitab Al-'Arab", p240

policy, controlled by a monarch or other head of state – that is to say, what remains in effect today in most countries of the world.

Arab Muslim exploits in the realm of governance are not isolated from historical contexts in which science and literature progressed, for it is the scientific, intellectual and philosophical foundations which empowered Arabs to refine the structure of governance, despite the fact that Arab Islamic history did not always subscribe to this format throughout its many ages. Arab creativity shone brightly here, despite various rulers' deviation from this particular structure, for the Arab intellectual continued to excel during both ages – those that abided by consultation (Shura) and those that didn't. I have previously detailed Arabs' contributions to the fields of science, literature and other fields of knowledge; and will publish these afresh in my book *The Injustice of Relatives*. [1]

Examples of Arab Muslim Contributions to the Field of Science

What is sometimes described as the first European university – the Schola Medica Salernitana – was established at the hands of Arabs in the Italian city of Salerno in around 840 CE. At that time, it was considered to be an extension of the Islamic universities in the East. It is worth noting that the graduates of these European universities would return triumphantly home after their success wearing Arab thobes and shirt, emulating the Muslims in their dress.

In those days, Arab dress signified a student's distinction and high social status because he had graduated from an Islamic university. The same tradition remains to this day, explaining the reason behind the flowing robes worn by graduates of Western universities among others. When speaking of this in his book *Islam in Europe*,

---

[1] Hamad bin AbdulAziz AlKawari, "The Injustice of Relatives", Hamad bin Khalifah University Press, 2019

Jack Goody says: "Arab dress as exemplified by the thobe remains the purest and most obvious symbol of academic integrity in our present day, particularly during significant moments such as the viva and during graduation day."

What is certainly vital to academic integrity is the process of peer review, a necessary and extremely important mechanism in scientific research. It is demonstrated when publishing research and studies in peer-reviewed journals and presenting them to the academic community – including scientists and researchers in other fields – in order to identify any existing deficiencies or to have it approved by the scientific community. Dr. Kiri Beilby, of Monash University in Melbourne, Australia, states that this practice originated in Arab culture when hadith scholars began to verify the authenticity of the noble hadith (prophetic traditions), as they were already presenting the hadith they had memorised to their counterparts in order to receive their opinions and ensure their veracity. This is how isnads (the chain of people from the time of Muhammad who can authenticate the veracity of a hadith) were born, and how hadith were categorised into irreproachable, weak, fabricated, successively narrated and so on.

Nowadays, when people are asked about the most influential scientists in the history of humanity, names such as Einstein, Galileo and Newton immediately spring to mind. However, rarely do they mention what these scientists owe their Arab predecessors from the 7th to the 14th centuries CE. This, unfortunately, is due to the veil obscuring the sight of intellectuals over the ages, which grew ever darker as a result of the ideology of hate towards Arab Muslims.

Dr. Beilby took the initiative to select 10 of the most prominent scientists who lived during the Golden Age of the Arabs, whilst Europe was experiencing an era of backwardness during the early Middle Ages, or the "Dark Ages" as labelled by the West. In this short list of the most significant scientists of the Arabian Golden Age, we find Abu 'Ali Al Hassan Ibn Al Haytham in 10th place, born in Basra, Iraq. He lived from 965 – 1040 CE and is considered to be a founder of today's modern science of optics. Ibn Al Haytham rejected Euclid's theory of optics and debunked both Ptolemy and Aristotle's hypotheses which claimed that "light either shone from the eye in order to illuminate the object in vision or emanated from within the object itself". Contrary to this, Ibn Al Haytham posited that light travelled towards the eye itself in rays from different points around any given object. This was the conceptual foundation of the science of optics. His book "Optics" was translated into Latin more than five times, and he was the first to think of regulating the flooding of the river Nile.

In ninth place, we have Ghayyathaldeen Abul Futuh, commonly known as Omar Khayyam (1048-1131 CE), mathematician and poet who was born in Nishapur in Iran. Amongst Khayyam's achievements was to calculate the length of the solar year precisely, down to ten decimal places. According to our contemporary computations, he was off only slightly, by a fraction of a second. His calculations were used to create a calendar which is considered to be more precise than the Gregorian calendar, which did not come into existence till 500 years later.

Muhammad bin Jabir Al Battani (858 – 929 CE) is listed in eighth position, who was born in Harran, Turkey. Although the Ancient Greeks were the first to theorise trigonometry, Al Battani was the first to develop and establish it as an independent branch of mathematics. He was also the first to establish the formulae linking lines and angles, for instance $\tan x = \sin$ of angle $x / \cos$ of x. The motivation behind his research and endeavours in this field was his desire to determine the direction of qibla (the direction Muslims must face when praying towards the Kaaba in Makkah) from any geographical location on earth.

They are followed by Abu Bakr Muhammad Al Razi in seventh place, researcher and physician who was born in Rayy near Tehran and lived from 865 – 923 CE. Al Razi identified fever as one of the body's defence mechanisms and was the first to describe the symptoms of smallpox and measles. He opened many doors of knowledge in medicine, surgery, philosophy and chemistry. His book "Kitab al-Hawi fi al-tibb" (The Comprehensive Book of Medicine), is one of his most prominent publications, in which he compiled a mighty encyclopaedia of medicinal knowledge that included many summaries of work penned by Greek and Indian authors in addition to his own observations and applied experiences. This book was translated into Latin in the 15th century; and remained the ultimate authority until the 17th century. Most of Al Razi's works were translated into European languages and were circulated until they became amongst the main sources of reference for Europe's most famous universities.

The sixth place is dedicated to the surgeon Abu Qasim Khalaf Al Zahrawy (936 – 1013), born in the Zahra'a in the suburbs of Cordoba in modern-day Spain. Al Zahrawy is considered to be one of the founding fathers of contemporary modern surgery. Amongst his many discoveries is the concept of using animal intestines (now commonly referred to as catgut) in the suturing of internal wounds, since they dissolve naturally and do not trigger adverse reactions from the body's immune system. Al Zahrawy is also famed for inventing a selection of surgical tools, including the obstetric surgeon's retractor used for widening a woman's vagina during the process of childbirth.

In fifth place, we find Abu Ja'afar Muhammad ibn Muhammad, also known as Nasir al Din Al Tusi (1202 – 1274) – astronomer, chemist and mathematician born in Tus, Iran. Famous for his accurate astronomical instruments and for his precise observations, he also separated the discipline of trigonometry from astronomy and composed astronomical tables which he called "Alzij Alikhani". These illustrated the movements of the planets with a high degree of accuracy and precision, so he relied on them to correct existing models that were inherited from the Roman astronomer

Ptolemy, describing the unified circular orbital movement of each planet around the sun. This work led one of his later students to discover that planets actually have an elliptical orbit. Subsequently, Copernicus was to rely on Al Tusi's work and that of his students without citing them or mentioning his sources.

In fourth place comes Ali Al Hussain ibn Sina, scholar and physician born in Bukhara, Uzbekistan (980 – 1037 CE). Commonly known as Avicenna in the western world, his contributions to the fields of physics, optics, philosophy and medicine were seminal; and his book "Al Qanun fil Tib" (The Canon of Medicine), represented a major reference for medical education in Europe until the 17th century CE. His discoveries include the nerve cells' responsibility for transmitting pain signals. His detailed study on the vectors and carriers of disease including soil, air, physical contact, proximity and sexual intercourse, had a profound impact on the medical profession. With his two articles on minerals and metals published in his book "Kitab Al Shifa'" (The Book of Healing), Ibn Sina is also considered to have laid the foundations of geology in the Arab world. He applied himself to this field, articulating concepts in sound scientific language, until the results of his research became the essential basis of European knowledge, and historical European encyclopaedists had no choice but to refer to his writings whenever they dealt with geology and the earth sciences.

Ala'addin Ali Al Qurashi, nicknamed Ibn Al-Nafis (1213 – 1288), comes in at third place. A surgeon and polymath, he was born in Damascus, Syria and authored the encyclopaedia titled "Al Shamil fil Sina'ah Al Tibiyyah" (The Comprehensive Book on Medicine). The prevailing opinion at that time was that blood was made in the liver and was then transported from there to the heart, then circulated in the veins. However, Ibn Al Nafis discovered microcirculation and wrote: "Blood is purified in the lungs in order for life to continue and to grant the body the ability to work; for the blood exits the right ventricle and goes to the lungs, where it mixes with the air then goes to the left ventricle."

The chemist Abu Musa Jabir ibn Hayyan (815 – 721 CE), who was born in in Kufa in Iraq during the Abbasid Dynasty ranks second. The French chemist Marcellin Berthelot says: "Indeed, Jabir ibn Hayyan is to chemistry what Aristotle is to logic." One of his most famous books is "The Seventy Epistles", which Gerard of Cremona translated into Latin in the year 1178 CE. Jabir ibn Hayyan is considered to be one of the founders of the scientific method in experimental sciences; and is credited with the discovery of sulphuric acid (which he called oil of vitriol), caustic soda and other acids.

First place is taken by the mathematician Muhammad ibn Musa Al Khawarizmi (781 – 850 CE), originally from Khawarizm in Iran. He is the original founder of algebra and was the first to use this term to describe the mathematical operations similar to equations which he created whilst trying to solve calculations for computing the inheritance system according to the Islamic system. He is the one who produced a comprehensive system of counting and arithmetic; and invented what are now called Arabic numerals from 0 to 9. It is a fact universally known that modern computers and digital products rely primarily on what are called "algorithms" (from the pronunciation of Al Khawarizmi), named after this eminent scholar.

Arabs' Contributions to the Arts, Humanities and Literature

Nations, just like individuals, have civilisational cycles, and they grow weaker or stronger according to specific conditions. Arabs are not alone in this world – they are an integral part, both being affected by it and having an impact on it. There is no doubt whatsoever that

Arabs are pioneers and take precedence in many fields that are today classified under the category of humanities. If we were to consider a discipline as critical as linguistics, for example, we would find that the Arab Muslims have excelled in establishing their language's grammar and that other cultures have benefited enormously from this. Everybody knows that Jewish linguists adopted the structure of Arabic grammar as a model on which to establish the parameters of the Hebrew language due to the similarities between the two sister tongues within the Semitic language tree.

The powerful influence of Islamic thought on Jewish thought is attested to by the most prominent Jewish thinker of the Middle Ages – Abu Imran Abu Musa ibn Maimun ibn 'Ubayd Allah Al Qurtubi (1135 – 1204 CE), who, when he moved to Fez in Morocco, studied at the hands of Muslims at the University of Al Qarawiyyin. He was greatly influenced by their writings, especially those of Ibn Rushd, whose work he continued to study for 13 years according to his own testimony. This is palpable in his surviving writings which are indications of a concerted exercise in Jewish philosophical and theological diligence. Amongst these are his treaties on the reconciliation of Jewish monotheism and philosophy within a vision that blends biblical interpretation with the science of theology. The philosophy of Ibn Rushd (who worked assiduously to highlight the connections between law and philosophy), had a marked influence on the writings of this Jewish theologian scholar. It is interesting to note that some Arab students considered Ibn Maimun to be an Islamic philosopher by virtue of his intellectual approach which closely resembles that of Islamic theology , regardless of the religious content of his writings and his positionality with regard to the prophethood of Muhammad the Messenger (peace be upon him), his call and his message. Over the course of many long centuries, his book "Guide of the Perplexed" gained a formidable standing amongst Jews knowledgeable in the field of philosophy as well as influencing their intellectual and cultural history in general.

Ibn Maimun (Maimonides in Hebrew) benefitted much from the fruits of Jewish co-existence with, and integration into, the Arab-Islamic context in Andalusia as it was fertile ground for religious thought and tolerance, because the cultural contexts in Islamic societies gave full rein to non-Muslims so their creativity may be nurtured. Here, it is essential to point out that the virtues of the Islamic civilisation towards other cultures were not limited only to the pioneering production of intellectual and scientific thought, but extended to something far greater which was the gift of a holistic socio-intellectual ethos, which nurtured intellectuals into creativity and facilitated the dissemination of their ideas.

It goes without saying that the role of Ibn Rushd (1126 – 1198) should be remembered here, and his influence on Western thought in general. This could be through the connections between him and the heritage of Greek logic forged through his expositions on Aristotle, or his distinguished presentation of the links between the temporal and religious for the sake of which he underwent much suffering during his life, with some contemporary scholars today viewing it as a contribution to the development of laicism. In all cases, Western medieval researchers were not mistaken in considering Ibn Rushd to be the philosopher with the greatest influence on Christian and Jewish thought, as well as the thought of those shaped by the European Renaissance, to the degree that they would call him the spiritual father of modern Western thought. In him, medieval philosophers found the best expositions of Aristotle's writings and came to recognise him as the epitome of an effective and persuasive defender of philosophy against its enemies and naysayers.

In reality, Ibn Rushd was nothing but the continuation of a philosophical and intellectual trend that had grown within Arab culture from the beginning, in a relationship that at that time combined the philosophical Greek quest for the universal with essential characteristics of Arab culture. For this very reason, Muslim philosophers such as Al-Farabi and Ibn Sina were not merely followers of Aristotelian philosophy by way of transmission, but rather they added much to it as a result of their expositions and commentaries on Aristotle's books on one hand, and by their translations into the Arabic language interlaced by Islamic virtues on the other.

A fascinating and intriguing debate arose between Arab grammarians and logicians around the use of language to demonstrate the connection between mind and speech, a culture in which the science of grammar developed astonishingly; in this Muslim Arabs adopted Greek logic, which they considered to be a model for all sciences. On it, they built its foundations and rested its pillars from which they would extrapolate the key concepts that gave rise to the formulation of scientific theories. It is a controversy that does not differ in any way from what modern-day philosophers of language deem to be a causal relationship between natural logic – everyday language that is used in daily speech – and manufactured, synthetic logic.

As for linguistics, Al Khalil ibn Ahmad Al Farahidi (718 – 791) collated the first dictionary of the Arabic language based on the order of the letters' phonetic pronunciation, from the final pharyngeal letter, the 'ayn, to the final bilabial, the meem – so he called it "The Book of 'Ayn". Al Khalil made great contributions to the linguistic sciences in general. He organised the science of Arabic prosody in a precise mathematical way and was cited by Sibawayh (760 - 796 CE), the prominent grammarian and scholar who was author of the first compendium on Arabic grammar "Al Kitab" (The Book), which included his opinions on the subject.

Many other works by Arab scholars involving the establishment of Arabic dictionaries followed, including Abu Mansour Al Azhari's (895 – 981 CE) "The Refinement of Language"; as well as Ismail Al

Jawhari's (940 – 1002 CE) "The Crown of Language and Perfection of Arabic", later to be known in short as "Al Sahih". Subsequently, "Lisan Al Arab" (The Tongue of Arabs) emerged, penned by the writer, historian and linguist Muhammad bin Manthur Al Ansari (1233 – 1311 CE). It is considered to be the most renowned and complete Arabic dictionary. However, whenever we pick up any book today that charts the history of language, its grammar and its structures, we find a neglected vacuum that corresponds directly to the period when the Arabic language ruled supreme as the world's lingua franca during the European Middle Ages. It is as if the science of linguistics did not exist amongst the Arabs, despite all that German, English and French Orientalists have written over the ages expounding on Arab linguistic achievements, whether they be grammar, dictionaries, rhetoric or otherwise. It is sufficient then for non-European ancient times to include Indian grammar, move onto Greek and Latin grammar and then leap to the areas that are familiar to the West today, completely ignoring the vacuum that spans many centuries, as if humanity had ceased all creativity in this branch of knowledge and its composite arts during this time.

The constructs of Hebrew grammar were modelled on the structure of Arabic grammar, yet Europeans disregard the impact of Arabic grammar on Hebrew during the Andalusian era. Arabic was taught in European universities in the 14th century and knowledge of its disciplines including grammar, morphology and rhetoric spilt over to the French school in the 17th century, thus impacting their own theories of language and continuing to impact European linguistic theory both directly and indirectly.

In reality, Westerners did not catch up with the science of linguistics until much later because they were unable to do so without benefitting from Arabic linguistic heritage given the differences between Arabic as the dominant lingua franca of the time and European languages which fall under the umbrella of Indo-European languages.

With reference to the classification of dictionaries for example, Westerners were not to learn this linguistic craft until many centuries later, when the first real dictionary in the Italian language came into existence in 1612 CE produced by the Accademia della Crusca. This was followed by a French language dictionary produced by L'Académie Française in 1694. The first English language dictionary – Samuel Johnson's *Dictionary of the English Language* – was not to appear until 1755 CE, and the *Oxford Dictionary of the English Language* followed more than 150 years later, in 1927 CE.

As for literature we can mention, for example, the philosopher-poet Abu Al'Ala'a Al Ma'arri and his work "Risalat Al Ghufran" (Message of Forgiveness) which is considered to be one of the greatest books of Arabic literary and critical heritage. It is a narration of a wonderful literary journey in which he converses with writers, poets and linguists in another realm which lies between Heaven and Hell. In this book of his, Al Ma'arri gleans descriptions of Paradise and Hellfire from his reading of the Qu'ran and takes inspiration from the miraculous journey of Al'isra' wal Mi'raj in order to construct his imaginary world. Al Ma'arri's book is a giant literary encyclopaedia, an enjoyable and astonishing journey replete with scenes that bring together the afterlife and life on earth.

The dialogues with poets, linguists and writers that Al Ma'arri imagines in the other world are considered to be an important source for the study of classical literary criticism, as these conversations and dialogue contain fundamentally important seminal topics in the subject in addition to the enjoyable and entertaining stories that they describe.

It is remarkable to note that two centuries after "Risalat Al Ghufran" was written, its influence comes to the surface in a near-identical work of literature, namely the poet Dante's "Divine Comedy", which Ruhi Al Khalidi describes as follows in his book "The History of the Literature of Franks and Arabs": "Amongst the Italians there emerged a poet, Dante (1265 – 1321 CE). His fame spread around the world, as he ranks amongst the greatest of poets in both ancient and modern nations. The reason for his fame is his book titled "The Divine Comedy" which he wrote in 1300 and divided into three sections: The Book of Hell, The Book of Purgatory and The Book of Paradise. Each section consists of 100 cantos, each canto containing 130 or 140 verses. He begins his work with the section on Hell and imagines himself approaching and overlooking a darkened forest, the description of which makes one's skin crawl. He makes as if to enter; and would truly have done so were it not for the presence of three predatory lions who accost his path. As he is between the jaws of death, Virgil, the Latin poet, appears unto him and offers to be his guide through Hell and Purgatory, simply because he is unable to enter Paradise or even to stand at its threshold because he is an idol worshipper. Dante accepts to be led by Virgil and they walk together in the world of the people of Hell. The poet vividly describes Hell's inhabitants and depicts the torment suffered by the oppressors and tyrants who he passes by. He comes to the story of Ugoline, a stubborn tyrant in the city of Pisa who fell into the hands of his enemies. They locked him up with his children in a tower and sealed all the exits. As his hunger intensified, he ate his children and then died. Dante's description of these scenes using dramatic literary style is phenomenal. When his final journey led him to Paradise, he found Beatrice at the gates. Beatrice was one of Florence's famous beauty queens. It was said that she was his lover, so she received him and together they penetrated the layers of Christian Paradise or the layers of Heaven, where they met many of the righteous, saints and archangels. He discussed matters pertaining to theology and divine sciences. In his work, Dante combined the literature, sciences and knowledge of his era and used them to lay the foundations of the Italian language. His book was like a circle of knowledge and literature, and it continues to stop writers in their tracks, attracting their attention with its excellent casting and careful arrangement as well as its unusually skilful navigation between one topic and the other. The Divine Comedy directly resembles "Risalat Al Ghufran", penned by Al Ma'arri more than two centuries prior to the existence of Dante's work. He had originally presented it as a response to a missive sent to him by one of his distinguished friends from Allepo."

This is one of the legacies of Arabic heritage that appeared during the Middle Ages, the impact of which emerged in Western culture after two centuries – each of these describing an amazing journey through other worlds.

We cannot ignore the great role that the book "A Thousand and One Nights" played in shaping Western narrative. Since its translation by the French orientalist Antoine Galland between 1704 and 1717 CE, it has been influencing the works of Western writers as well as others. When we read the works of Shakespeare, we are drawn by how markedly he was influenced by "A Thousand and One Nights" in his play "The Tempest" or by the impact that it had on Robert Louis Stevenson's "Treasure Island". In fact, the British orientalist Arberry goes so far as drawing parallels between Shakespeare's "Othello" in which Othello the Moor suffocates his wife Desdemona because he suspects her of being unfaithful, and Qamar Al Zaman with his beloved. We also find influences of "A Thousand and One Nights" in Italian literature, in the famed "Decameron", or "Ten Nights" by the writer Giovanni Boccaccio. Similarly, its influences on German literature are evident in the works of Goethe, where the events in "Lover's Mood" closely mirror Amina's story in "A Thousand and One Nights", to the extent that Goethe preserves her name in his narrative and uses the story of "Abu Hassan and the Daylight Sun" as the source of his ideas regarding marriages of the bourgeoisie class in Germany. Likewise, the second act of his play "Faust" contains much of the content to be found in the story of "Prince Amir and Durrat Al Kawaz".

Gabriel García Márquez did not hide the extent to which he was influenced by "A Thousand and One Nights", for its magical narrative greatly nurtured the writer's imagination and stretched his horizons. Studies of comparative literature bear witness to how a number of other writers were influenced by this work and that it became a source of inspiration by virtue of its stories that brought together content from ancient civilisations and were written by a Muslim Arab mind at the very pinnacle of Abbasid civilisation. "A Thousand and One Nights" reached other creative outlets other than literature, for it inspired musicians including Rimsky Korsakov in 1888 who demonstrated creative brilliance in his piece "Scheherazade" as influenced by The Nights, as well as Carl Nielsen and his "Aladdin Suite" in 1918, in addition to the choreography of various animated films.

We spoke of Al Ma'arri the poet, and he is the descendant of a civilisation that took much pride in its supremacy when it came to poetry, even prior to the advent of Islam. And we spoke of "A Thousand and One Nights" – these are two prominent examples of the power of Arabic literature's influence as well as its impact on humanity in general.

However, Arabic culture is replete with unique characteristics that have contributed to the enrichment of humanity. Amongst these is an unparalleled phenomenon the Arabs call "Al Mua'llaqat" to this day, obliquely referring to festooned precious necklaces; the Arabs would write the most perfect of poems in the age of Jahiliyyah (pre-Islamic Arabia) using gold water and hang them on the coverings of the noble Ka'abah. These were considered to be the epitome of the Arabs' lived experience and the most perfect manifestation of their literary expression, in order that they would be engraved in people's memories just as securely as the necklaces were fastened. The strong links between poetry and the esoteric experiences of spirituality are well known, particularly considering its connection with rhythm and music.

It is because the Arabs had knowledge of the science of meter through which the brilliant linguist Al Khalil bin Ahmad set rhythms derived from the very heart of the Arabic language, that the discipline of music gradually evolved and became more intimately connected to poetry. Many great works bear witness to this significant influence, such as Al-Isfahani's "Kitab Al-Aghani" (Book of Songs) and the works of great philosophers such as Abu Nasr Al-Farabi, author of "The Great Book of Music", who had the title Second Teacher, as he was thought to be second only to Aristotle in his knowledge. Shaykh Ibn Sina, in his book "Al-Shifa'a" (The Cure), referred to the use of music as a treatment for the soul, as was also mentioned in Al-Kindi's treatise "Madkhal Sina't Al Musiqah" (An Introduction to the Making of Music). We find in Al-Ghazali's "Ihya' 'Ulum Al Din" (Revival of the Religious Sciences): "Whomsoever Spring does not move, nor its flowers – the oud and its strings, is corrupt of temperament and disposition; and there is no cure for them." It appears that the legacy Al-Farabi left behind in his work "The Great Book of Music" in terms of his vision for the future of music-making enriched Western music theories. He dived deeply, coming up with expressive, profound analyses that led him to formulate and establish an aesthetic theory defining the standards of musical beauty, enriching Western theories of music. By virtue of Arab contributions, Western music was able to break through and access many genres such church singing, lyrical poetry, tragic opera and tragic lyrical poetry, which they inherited as traditions from the Greeks and the Romans.

The increased interest in music, its instruments, philosophical principle and means of development, led to many decisive theoretical contributions throughout the history of global music theory; including the establishment of musical notation, measurement of tones and times, and formulation of the musical scale, which facilitated the development of melodies, methods of musical performance and the manufacture and intonation of the instruments themselves.

But what concerns us most in this regard is that these achievements within the Arabic-Islamic space were then transferred to countries that were outside the Arab-Islamic Empire. This is a page in history where much cross-cultural interaction took place, where civilisations and their arts intertwined. Much has been written on this, which shows that these influences were passed on through three geographical gateways – Andalusia, Sicily and Turkey during the eras of their Islamic rule. The archives groan under the weight of many illustrated manuscripts which bear witness to the churches' use of Arabic musical instruments starting from the rule of the Frankish king Charlemagne (724 – 814 CE), such as percussion, tabla, trumpet, horn, violin, oud, rebab and others. Since the 19th century, some comparative theories suggest that the songs and poems of the troubadours in the 12th century CE were not devoid of the influence of Arabic poetry and music, especially the muwashahat and zajal genres. Whatever the corresponding theories may be, the close geographical proximity and marked dominance of Andalusian culture during the Middle Ages undoubtedly had significant impact on the travelling musicians and troubadours in France, Germany, England, Italy, Portugal and Spain – whether from the perspective of the muwashahat and the recital of various stories from "A Thousand and One Nights", "Yusuf and Zuleikha" or as a consequence of creating and refining new syllabic weights, then dividing them into strings and segments similar to muwashahat in terms of rhythm and verse, in addition to blending poetry and music in the muwashahat style.

In truth, this Arab-Islamic interest in music is a single manifestation of a holistic philosophical world view that encompasses music as a single element. If we consider that the Islamic conception is based entirely on the fact that a Muslim worships Allah alone with no partner, then this servant of the Lord will view helping others as a form of personal worship. As a result, all available means that will lead to the happiness of humankind, their comfort and enjoyment subsequently becomes a religious duty through which the Muslim receives the best reward from his Creator.

Influence and Favour

Researchers and those involved in comparative studies have often been interested in studying the influence of Arab civilisation in the West on the fields of theoretical and rational sciences such as logic, philosophy and theology, as well as the fields of mathematical sciences like arithmetic, algebra, engineering, and astronomy, in addition to the fields of the natural sciences such as physics, chemistry, zoology and botany. They did not, however, delve deeply into the influence that Arab literature had on Western literature, and this is an important area in the history of Arab civilisation and the light that it shed on the world, just as it is evidence of the depth of interaction and dialogue between Arabic literature and the literature of other foreign peoples.

As the Spanish orientalist Angel González Valencia acknowledged: "The Arab poetic structure has become a vehicle for expressing the feelings of different peoples and in different languages. We must add it to the glories of the immortal Arab civilisation which spread to Europe by way of the Muslim Spaniards… in any case, whenever we recall the heritage that Spanish Muslims brought with them and added to European civilisation, we feel proud because those who left us these masterpieces of art – zajal, muwashahat, philosophical theories on which Western thinkers were raised; and the books of science and medicine that contributed to making life into something far better and more beautiful, those who reached the pinnacle of civilisations during their time by making Spain the most cultured and refined country in Europe – these were the ancestors of our race; and it is an injustice to strip them of their 'Spanishness' simply because they were Muslims."[1]

Valencia continues, saying that Andalucian poetry's influence reached French, English and Italian poetry "and the style of this type of Andalusian poetry – by this I mean zajal and muwashahat – remained in the creation of musical melodies throughout the Middle Ages... and in French folk songs...and even in England we come across old poetic songs dedicated to the Virgin Lady Mary that are sung during Christmas celebrations that have all been poured from the same Andalusian mould. To this very day, we still find traditional Scottish and Irish folk songs arranged according to the quatrains of the Islamic Andalusian zajals." [2]

Arabic poetry reached Spanish poetic circles, and the Spaniards became hugely enamoured of it. Muhammad Kurd Ali writes in clarification: Historical Spanish ballads and sonnets in which feast days, ring games, bull fighting, gymkhana and knights dancing are described are all imitations or translations from the Arabic. The Spanish did not invent anything in this vein prior to the 15th century. It is this circumstance that caused the Arabs of Spain to become famous throughout the entirety of Europe. Spain's poet Francisco Villaespesa said: "No nation has been afflicted with the divine gift of poetry as much as the Arab people have." [3]

We cannot disregard the composition of King Saiko IV's court – which brought together 13 Arab poets and 12 Western poets – nor the spread of troubadour poetry as a result of the wandering minstrels who would later go forth and travel throughout the Spanish Provence, influenced by this Arabic poetry. That is not

---

1   Angel González Valencia "Andalusian Poetry and its influence on European Poetry" tr. Dr. Al-Tahir Makki in his book "Andalusian Studies in Literature, History and Philosophy" p 200
2   Op.cit. p 194 -195
3   Muhammad Kurd Ali, "Islam and Arab Civilisation" Dari Hindawi, first edition 2017 p214

to mention that their very names are directly extracted from the Arabic language, for "troub" comes from the word "tarab" and "dour" from "adwar", thus creating a term for poet-singers who sing lyrical poetry. They benefitted greatly from the Andalusian zajal and muwashahat, to the extent that some of their verses match up with Arabic poetry directly.

Although I believe that Andalusian poetry had a major influence on Western poetry in general, and even on music at that time, the architectural evidence that towers tall in Spain is, alone, sufficient to acknowledge the reality of this influence, which came about as a result of dialogue and the ability of Muslim Arabs to influence Spanish architecture both before and after the fall of Granada. Our best example here is the prevalence of Mudéjar architecture in the Middle Ages.

There is no doubt, then, that there exist many diverse examples demonstrating the influence of Arab literature on world literature, not only Western literature. When I raise this point, I do not mean to claim a monopoly or state that Arab literature is the only element to have had an influence on the literary output of these societies. Rather, I adhere to the principles of reciprocity and cross-fertilisation amongst other cultures; just as our writings have impacted those of others, so ours has been influenced by them in different eras. I am simply highlighting this in order to protest the cultural fanaticism that announces the purity of its own literature and culture and claims it to be free from all external influences or perceives other cultures to be inferior and undeserving of dialogue – an attitude which is destined to end up sowing hatred.

The Arabs did not deny the favours of others towards their civilisation and there can be no justification for denying the favours of Arabs towards humankind. Our heritage and cultural history are replete with realities where the Arab has benefited from the symbolic goodness of other civilisations, even in a state of civilisational clash. This is clearly conveyed to us, for example, by the Egyptian historian Al-Jabarti's report written during the time of the French campaign against Egypt. Here, he describes the Egyptian students' avid passion for reading, learning and their interaction with the books presented by the French: "They (the scholars of Napoleon's campaign against Egypt) were made known to administrators, astronomers and people of knowledge and to the mathematical sciences such as engineering, architecture and drawing, vocations such as engravers, photographers, scribes, arithmeticians and artisans in a new residential street located in the neighbourhood of Al-Nasiriyyah... They took one of the houses and placed a large collection of their books in it – that is to say, they converted it into a public library. They also appointed a librarian and officials to care for it and to fetch the volumes that the students required. The students gather there every day, two hours before noon and they sit in the courtyard of the place, opposite the bookstores on chairs and seating set up parallel to the wide, rectangular table. The student would then request whatever he would like to peruse and the official responsible for the store would bring it to him. In this manner, even the lowliest of soldiers would browse, leaf through the volumes and write. Should a Muslim arrive, wishing to take a look too, they would not prevent him from entering this, the dearest of places to them. No, they would greet him with smiles and demonstrate happiness at his arrival, especially if they notice that he has an interest in general knowledge, an inclination to learning or a curiosity to discover. In this case, they demonstrate much love and affection and they immediately ply him with all sorts of books of different genres – geography of the regions, animals, birds, plants, histories of ancient nations, their narrations of stories of the prophets, their miracles, signs and the events that befell their people – an array that would baffle the thoughts."[1]

---

1. Abdulrahman bin Hassan Al-Jabarti, "Tarikh 'Ajaib Al-Athar fi Al-tarajim wal Akhbar", Dar Al-Jil, Beirut, vol.2 p 234

From the Past Towards the Future

No wise, knowledgeable person would deny that Arab culture is ancient and that it has seriously contributed to human civilisation with its various achievements, as we have seen in the short list of polymath Arab scholars who distinguished themselves in most fields of knowledge. The intention behind this quick snapshot is not to glorify the past of a civilization that dominated the global scene for centuries with its knowledge, literature and other manifest contributions to humanity. By this reminder, we only intend to link the past with the present and to demonstrate that contemporary Western civilisation did not spontaneously spring into existence as a result of the miracles of Western man alone. Rather, it is a single episode out of human civilisation's many and the product of global human development in which previous peoples and civilisations contributed – amongst them is the Arab-Islamic which we claim provided the scientific, philosophical and intellectual foundations of the European Renaissance in a way unmatched by any other civilisations. This is not a form of arrogance, but legitimate pride based on our roots, our identity, our heritage and our cultural capital.

During their first renaissance in the Middle Ages, the Muslim Arabs did not hesitate to glean wisdom that would help them flourish from the Indian and Persian civilisations. The Europeans also took from our civilisations in order to build their own modern renaissance and now we all, Arabs and Westerners and nations from across the world, do not belong to the Western civilisation. Instead, we belong to a contemporary human civilisation, for this civilisation is not limited to a single geographic area nor is it the product of the contributions of one single civilisation. It is the product and legacy of the complex and intertwined efforts of humanity.

This understanding allows us to unfurl the banner of dialogue with the Other, because we do not believe that the values of contemporary society and its technological, scientific and intellectual products are at odds with our identity. But does the West share this understanding with us? And does it interact with us and with other nations that belong to ancient civilisations with equity and respect?

Certainly, discounting the Arab bloc when administering global cultural affairs via an organisation whose very foundations are built on humanity's shared values appears to be part of disregarding this ancient civilisation's contributions. Contributions that paved the way for the ideas which shaped our civilisational reality today; ideals on which UNESCO was founded and strives to embody whilst empowering all nations to enjoy their shared history, diversity, multiplexity and similarity of the spectrum of cultures and heritages.

It is clear that these achievements are not limited to the glorious past to which cultural monuments bear witness till this very day, as they point to the lofty position of the Arabic civilisation. The representative list of the World Heritage Sites, which are supervised by UNESCO, show that Arab countries have many such sites. Indeed, there are 83 cultural heritage sites in the Arab world. Seven are in Algeria, seven in Egypt, five in Iraq, three in Palestine, six in Lebanon, five in Libya, one in Mauritania, nine in Morocco, five in Oman, one in Qatar, six in Saudi Arabia, two in Sudan, five in Jordan, three in Bahrain, six in Syria, seven in Tunisia, one in the United Arab Emirates and four in Yemen.

Likewise, Arab countries contribute significantly to the Representative List of Intangible Human Heritage through various diverse crafts and customs including Arabic coffee, falconry, the Arab majlis, the date palm tree and other elements of authentic Arab cultural heritage that the whole world acknowledges.

When researchers seriously enquire about the source of this tangible and intangible heritage, they find satisfactory answers in the history of the Arab region. Leading experts in history, art history and archaeology acknowledge without ambiguity the astonishing richness of the many waves of civilisation that have washed over the Arab region, one by one from the Arabian Gulf to the Atlantic Ocean. In Yemen, there are traces of the history of religions harking from the Kingdom of Sheba, of which the world has continued to speak through the ages. Not far from there is Mesopotamia, land of the two rivers where mighty civilisations flourished, including the Kingdom of the Sumerians, the Kingdom of the Akkadians, the Kingdom of the Babylonians and the Kingdom of the Assyrians – the remnants of which to this day continue to dazzle human minds and bear witness to civilisational sophistication in culture, architecture, law, arts and thought. In this self-same Arab region, the great Phoenician civilisation also appeared which gifted humanity the letters of the alphabet.

We are duty bound not to exaggerate in glorifying the achievements of these civilisations but at the same time we cannot underestimate their role and influence. The civilisations of the Near East came into being and looked out onto the world more than 3,000 years before the sun rose on the Ancient Greek civilisation. The Greek civilisation benefited from these civilisations' wealth of knowledge, as it was not an insular culture. Thus, its scholars and philosophers learned from the wisdom and sciences of the East. Let us remember Thales (d.547 BCE), who journeyed to Egypt in order to learn mathematics and geometry and benefited from the Babylonians' knowledge of astronomy. Pythagoras, too, who was born around 580 BCE and drew from the sciences of the East and imbibed philosophy and music during his travels. Plato (d. 347 BCE) and Democritus (d. 356 BCE) – two indomitable philosophers, the impact of Eastern wisdom on whom no serious or objective researcher can deny.

If we recall the Carthaginian civilisation, we will notice that the initial signs of representative democracy appear in it for the first time several centuries before its emergence in Athens, through the Council of Elders, which represented the various social classes.

It was Carthage itself that produced 28 volumes establishing the sciences of agriculture that was inherited by the Romans, with which they developed their own civilisation in turn. An honest researcher cannot fail to point out that the three Abrahamic faiths, namely Judaism, Christianity and Islam, appeared in the geographical space that represents the Arab world in our present time. As for the Pharaonic civilisation, to whose achievements the pyramids, palaces and temples testify, it is sufficient for us to read what the laureate Naguib Mahfouz said in this regard before the Nobel Academy when receiving the prestigious literary award: "I am the son of two civilisations that were, in an era of history, co-joined in a serendipitous marriage. The first is 7,000 years old – the Pharaonic civilisation; and the second is 1,400 years old – the Islamic civilisation. Perhaps I do not need to introduce either of the two civilisations to you, as you are the knowledgeable elite, but there is no harm in reminders, and we are in the business of seeking and learning. As for the Pharaonic civilisation, I will not speak of the invasions, conquests or the building of empires for these are threadbare feats that modern consciences are, thank God, uncomfortable recalling. Neither will I speak of her (Egypt's) damascene conversion to Allah the Almighty for the first time and the breaking dawn of human conscience, for this is a long narrative and there is not one amongst you that is not familiar with King Akhenaten. Nor will I talk about its achievements in the arts, literature and its famous miracles – the pyramids, the Sphinx and Karnak; for whoever has not been fortunate enough to witness these antiquities first hand has at least read about them and contemplated photographs of them. As the fates that are concerned with my personal situation have decided that I should be a storyteller, permit me to present the pharaonic civilisation to you in the guise of a story. Please do grace me by listening to this historical event.

"The pages of papyrus tell the tale of a Pharaoh who came to hear of a sinful relationship occurring between ladies of the harem and men of the court. It was expected that his punishment would befall on them all, in order that no-one would dare to deviate from the standards of moral behaviour at that time. However, he summoned an elite group of jurists to his presence and asked them to investigate what had come to his knowledge, informing them that he wished to know the truth of the matter in order that he may issue a fair verdict and rule with justice.

This behaviour, in my opinion, is greater than building an empire or constructing the pyramids; and is far more indicative of the superiority of civilisation than any pomp or wealth. This empire has dissipated and become part of the past. The pyramids, too, will disappear one day. But truth and justice will remain for as long as humanity has an aspiring consciousness and a conscience that is awake. With regard to the Islamic civilisation, I will not tell you about its invitation to establish the unity of humanity within The Creator's realm based on freedom, equity, tolerance and co-existence. Nor will I speak to you of the greatness of its Messenger, for some of your thinkers have paid homage to him as the greatest man in the history of humanity – nor will I describe its conquests that planted thousands of minarets calling people to goodness, piety and worship across lands stretching far and wide –from India to China to the borders of France. Neither will I highlight the strong bonds of inter-religious brotherhood that were realised between and within various faiths in the lands that were embraced by its rule, demonstrating a tolerance that humanity has never known before or since. But I will encapsulate it in one dramatic and moving situation that I would like to present to you, which distils one of its most prominent virtues. Following a battle against the Byzantine state in which the Egyptians were victorious, prisoners of war were returned in exchange for a number of books on philosophy, medicine and mathematics from the Ancient Greek heritage. This is a precious testimony to the human spirit and its constant striving and aspiration in the realms of knowledge and science, despite the fact that the seeker here is one who professes to follow a unitarian heavenly faith and the knowledge they seek is the fruit of a "pagan" civilisation." [1]

Naguib Mahfouz was entirely correct in considering the fruits of civilisation to be a source of nourishment for all humanity, as long as shared common values rise above differences, which have turned from elements of positive cultural diversity into pretexts for racial discrimination and the sowing of societal discord in various colonialist guises over the centuries.

This awareness that Mahfouz demonstrated does not mean that it is universally present amongst Arab intellectuals, regardless of their backgrounds. Rather, we do not deny that this level of awareness remains well out of reach for the Arab elite who have yet to awaken from the stupor of their ideological coma and their exaggerated, polarised conflict with the technologically modern West on one hand and the traditionalists on the other.

More importantly, despite its great value and the international community's adoption of the principle of cultural universality for human beings, is that the Arab bloc today has, perhaps, a far greater need than that of the other groups to engage deeply with the major universal questions that humanity poses to itself. Throughout the Arab world, the train of modernity has progressed at an astonishing speed; and many of the issues that Arabs pose to themselves have taken on a dangerous nature, such as the issue of identity, cultural and religious autonomy and the extent to which this relates to global transformations and globalisation. Prior to laying the foundations for a modern renaissance, let us begin with the reform and development of education so that it may become a powerhouse for nurturing human capital and the deployment of intelligence towards comprehensive development. For education

---

1   Nobel Literature Prize Winner's Lectures, 1985-1999 tr. Abdulwadud Al'Imrani, Aldar Al-Arabi for science publications, first edition, 2012 p175 -176

is perceived by most Arabs as the key to progress and the means by which they keep apace with the current movements of history; for example its relationship with heritage and its role in shaping cultural identity, its openness to the universal and the linking of its historical connection with other cultures in order to detract from the illusion of cultural self-sufficiency.

Arab intellectuals have touched upon the questions of the Renaissance since the end of the 19th century. There were questions mixed with concerns about benefiting from humanity's heritage. Here, we remember Al-Sanusi's statement during his Hijaz journey: "It is entirely logical for a person to allow themselves to be led by (or to emulate) others in that which brings them benefit." [1] Civilisation was the goal of all reformers who believed that the fruit of justice was 'umran – (the enlivening of civilisations). Al-Tahtawi called for humanitarian values to become a foundation for 'umran in his statement: 'Umran requires two great forces, one being a ruling force that brings benefits and repels detriment or corruption and the second the governed force which is the entity that has attained complete freedom and enjoys public benefits that provide all that a person needs" [2] Ibn Abi Al-Diyaf concurred with this position of Al-Tahtawi's by saying; "Whomsoever would like to read a valuable work in this vein should read the third chapter of the brilliant Egyptian Shaykh Muhammad Rifa'ah Al-Tahtawi's second article which he wrote during his trip to Paris and titled 'Talkhis Al-Ibriz fi Talkhis Paris' (The Extrication of Gold in Summarizing Paris), as he elegantly and masterfully summarises French legislature in a way that truly attests to his objectivity and fairness. In this chapter, he says: 'We relate this unto you – even if most of its contents are not

---

[1] Muhammad AlSanoussi, The Hijaz Journey ed. Ali AlShenoufi, Tunisian distributors, Tunis, first edition, 1976, pp117-118

[2] Rifa'ah Rafi' Al-Tahtawi, Manahij Al-Albab Al-Masriyyah in his collected works, ed. Muhammad Emara, The Arab Foundation for Research and Publication, Beirut, first edition, 1973, pp 516-517

in the Book of God Almighty, nor in the Sunnah of His Messenger, may Allah bless him and grant him peace – so that you may come to know how their minds decided that justice and fairness are amongst the reasons essential for the development of kingdoms and comfort of the people; and how both rulers and subjects were led by this principle until their countries were enlivened, their cultural capital increased, their wealth accumulated and their hearts rested and at ease. So, you do not hear one of their people complain, as justice is the bedrock of 'umran.'" [1]

The reformers and pioneers of the Arab Renaissance were not against using the achievements of modern Western civilisation, nor were they embarrassed by it and there is no doubt that they would have continued their flow until now, because what preoccupied the Arabs during the Renaissance era is exactly the same as what preoccupies contemporary Arab intellectuals, which is what elites around the world have pledged and that international organisations are founded upon, because shared values are the bedrock of renaissance.

These concerns, and many others, are at the core of UNESCO's missions; and preoccupy many thinkers who are united by their belief in its principles and values. We have always believed that granting the opportunity to one of the sons of this Arab bloc to head UNESCO would undoubtedly contribute to the advancement of the current discussions between Arab thinkers and their counterparts around the world in a way that facilitates the beneficial use of UNESCO literature. It would also pose afresh, on a global scale, the questions that often seem esoteric, thus achieving the desired rapprochement between cultures and establishing difference and diversity on a vision of human rights that contributes towards the removal of unrest and preconceived stereotypes. This would throw open avenues to reawaken hope in a vision that matches the lived

---

1   Ahmad bin Abi Al-Dayyaf, 'Ithaf ahl al-zaman bi akhbar muluk Tunis wa 'ahd al-aman, Al-Dar Al-Tunisi for publication, Tunis second edition 1976, vol.1 pp44-64

reality of Arabs, Muslims and their culture instead of reducing them to everything that opposes the principles of international peace and exposing them to the incitement of hatred and violence that makes the Arabs feel culturally inferior. People are not fated to submit to backwardness, deteriorating social conditions, political tyranny, or cultural, educational and scientific decline. Rather, these are all challenges that can and should be faced for the sake of a more beautiful and better tomorrow. Arabs, like all other nations, deserve a decent life and in a distinguished cultural context that interacts with universal values and human principles easily and in a straightforward manner.

This perception came as a result of my belonging to one of the great cultures in the history of humanity – one that has made magnificent contributions throughout the ages – and is based on my belief that the peoples of the Arab region yearn – just as other peoples in the world do – for freedom, for an authentic, sophisticated culture, for a deservedly free, dignified and decent life where they partake of humanity's concerns and enjoy the fruits of knowledge and philosophy. These are but some of the reasons that motivated me to run for the position of director-general of an organisation that is open to many cultures and built on one key principle – reforming minds in order to build lasting peace; minds that are capable of bringing peoples and cultures together on the basis of unified universal foundations whilst simultaneously respecting diversity and difference.

The wager was not one made by me personally as much as it was a wager on the extent to which the sons of Arab heritage themselves would support a proposition that would benefit humanity as a whole, as well as benefit themselves so that they may set out with strong, renewed hope for a safer, more beautiful and more reassuring world with no arrogance or inferiority complexes. There is no better school than UNESCO, the school of both difference and unity, to be the launchpad for such new hope, especially since the State of

Qatar – which nominated me for the position – shines brilliantly on the international stage, commands the confidence of global partners and has accumulated experience in successfully executing major civilisational projects with ample capabilities and resources. More significantly, its approach is one of sincerity and as a result, its demonstrably sincere intentions greatly facilitate all the above and harness them towards the empowerment of an Arab to lead an international cultural organisation of the stature of UNESCO. I am fortunate to have been that delegate. That is why I simultaneously considered both the sacrifice and the adventure as experiences that were worthy of pursuing right to the very end – to challenge myself, to honour my homeland, to act justly towards the Arab bloc and, finally, at the culmination of it all – to serve humanity.

Chapter Four
Soft Power

*"My brother – should Jupiter present you with a gift,
beware of taking anything from his hand."*

What is not Overcome by Coercion is won Over by Gentleness

Researchers' analyses demonstrate that soft power depends on two mechanisms, one of which belongs to the realm of reason and that is persuasion; whereas the other belongs to the realm of emotions and the essence of being, and that is temptation. As defined by Joseph S. Nye, political scientist and former United States Assistant Secretary of Defence for International Security Affairs: "It [soft power] is the ability to get what you want by attraction rather than coercion or financial outlay. This ability arises from a country's attractiveness, its political principles and policies. When our policies appear legitimate in the eyes of others, our soft power expands." [1] That is why "temptation" or "attraction" is the best way to accrue soft power, for winning people over is not at all an easy matter and it is an approach that requires strong arguments to achieve compliance. One is perfectly capable of influencing people by

---

1 Joseph S. Nye, Soft Power: The means to success in world politics, tr. Muhammad Tawfiq AlBayjarmi, ed. AbdulAziz Abdulrahman AlThanian, Dar Al'Abaikan, first edition 2007 p10

brute force, dictating the type of behaviour that must be followed, but the influence of soft power enables one to shape behaviour according to what is required until a stage is reached where it appears that this behaviour is entirely voluntary and results from faith and conviction, not from arbitrariness or coercion.

It is interesting to note what Nye said in his distinction between hard power and soft power as he cited the soft power possessed by the Vatican as an example to clarify his definitions. Stalin once mocked the Vatican saying: "How much military power does the Pope possess?" Whilst the Soviet Union was haemorrhaging influence due to its gradual loss of soft power, it was expanding militarily in Hungary and Czechoslovakia, but Stalin paid no heed to the extent of the real loss. On the other hand, the example set by an Indian Foreign Minister was striking and demonstrated his awareness of the overwhelming influence of soft power. When the Taliban government fell in 2001, the minister rushed to Kabul on board a plane to congratulate the interim government. This plane was not loaded with equipment or weapons. It was loaded with Bollywood films and music that were then subsequently distributed throughout Kabul, the country's capital.

I tend to agree with Nye's division of soft power, with it being based on a complex trilogy of elements, namely culture and political principles which apply domestically and abroad as well as foreign policy which overrides moral values. Naturally, culture is divided into what is often termed "elite culture" and "populist culture" and in analysts' opinions, elite culture is more able to infiltrate the lives of the populace. It is capable of penetrating to the level of the individual and transforming into behaviour, with connections to literature, art and education.

Despite its power of instant attraction, it does not necessarily leave positive results behind, in fact it often produces a sort of conflict, for the consumption of pizza could not change the leader of North Korea's behaviour; and the Rwandans would wear T-shirts emblazoned with American slogans and designs whilst engaged in armed combat with each other.

The United States of America has at its disposal, cultural values that have influenced many countries around the world. We have only to look at the majority of Nobel Prize winners – many of them are Americans; let us look to the medical, scientific and technological discoveries – a high percentage of their sources are American. Let us also look at education – did the United States not support and underwrite the process of changing educational curricula in Egypt years ago, an initiative which inevitably falls under the policy of soft power?

The United States of America became aware of the influence of soft political power very early on. However, we cannot avoid stating that soft power is the result of accumulated layers of ideas and policies that have been applied over the years in the face of various international situations, starting in the 1990s with the United States' policy of dual containment to deal with hostile regimes. The United States came to realise that its use of hard power at the expense of soft power led to the erosion of its moral standing, thus distorting its political and diplomatic image. This is what happened during its war on Iraq in 2003. Opinions swung towards a rejection of American intervention and opprobrium of American policy. However, this did not lessen peoples' attachment to American films, American music or any other American cultural products.

Following this, American experts preferred to return to those successful policies which they had used during the Cold War, which resulted in the demise and fall of the Soviet Union without a single bullet being fired. That is why both domestic and foreign political principles are defined by the extent of soft power's failure or success.

Hence, soft power has been harnessed in many different arenas including education, childcare, human relations, politics, and diplomacy to give but a few examples. An enlivening anecdote mentioned by Imam Al Ghazali in his book "Kitab Al 'Ilm" in relation to the requisite soft power involved in the teaching of boys, is that he would promise them clubs, birds and time to play with balls, or other similar pastimes that were tempting and attractive to them. Otherwise, without them, they would not have been motivated to study and work would have been burdensome and boring for them.[1]

The matter is no different when it comes to adults, since the human soul is at ease with that which makes it happy; and this explains the efforts of Allah's Messenger, peace be upon him, who always strove to improve relations between people, teaching us "tahadu tahabu"[2]– (exchange presents so that you may love one another more). He exhorted us to present gifts, for this is a thoughtful gesture that human souls generally warm towards, opening up to the giver and becoming more at ease with them.

The Diplomacy of Gifts

The anthropologist Marcel Mauss is considered to be amongst the first to conduct research into the concept of gifting in human societies, in an attempt to understand the phenomenon holistically from multiple perspectives and uncover the motivations that caused a significant number of the world's civilisations to organise their exchanges and contracts on its basis. He concluded that gifting reveals three processes. These are giving, receiving and reciprocating with a gift that is of equal or greater value. These processes take

---

1   Abu Hamid Al-Ghazali, Ihya' 'Ulum Al-Din, The Book of Knowledge, chapter four (The reasons behind motivations for studying, an introduction to disagreements, detailing the negative traits of munadharah and debating, as well as the conditions for its permissibility). "We it not for the promise of recreational time playing with balls, clubs and birds, boys would never have desired to study."

2   "exchange presents so that you may love one another more" – narrated by Al-Bukhari, in Al-Adab Al-Mufrad, as did Malik, verified by Al-Albani

place between two parties – the donor and the recipient – within a framework of solidarity and acceptance of sharing, which may bestow upon the donor a preferential position. As much as this process demonstrates a type of generosity, similarly, it may be described as a form of coercion as it obliges the recipient to reciprocate with a gift also.

Mauss began to dig around in the annals of ancient civilisations' histories in order to discover more about the different types of presents and their impact on societies. This is when he came across the phenomenon of "potlatch" practiced by the Indians of British Columbia at the end of the 19th century. Wealthy tribes used to practice potlatch during their celebrations during which the tribal leaders would compete. The leader of the tribe donates copious amounts of his wealth and precious possessions in order to prove his generosity, thus suffering a huge loss as a result of the constraints placed on him by this tradition. These losses continue and are perpetuated amongst the Kwakiutl tribes to the extent that many destroyed their own homes and crops, often burning them down so they could demonstrate their high status; for the more wealth is given and the more possessions are destroyed during these ceremonies, the more prestigious a rank the chieftain has.

Even though Mauss sought to delve deeply into Western history; and particularly primitive history, he did not seek to study the concept of gifting in Eastern societies generally, or the Arab Muslim civilisation in particular, even though he may have perfunctorily mentioned it in passing with reference to chapter 64 (Al Taghabun) in the Qur'an.[1] He focused mainly on its economic and societal aspects whilst generally disregarding the elements of

---

1   See Marcel Mauss, Research on Giving – Forms and methods of giving in Ancient societies, tr. AlMawladi Al-Ahmar, ed. 'Arous AlZubayr, The Arab Organisation for Translation, first edition, 2011, p240

positive reciprocity that occur as a result of gifting, for this is the main benefit that both the donor and recipient share.

Despite the interest in the "gift" and its manifestations in Western culture, specialist Western writings ignored the wealth of Arab experience, leading to the Arab civilisation becoming oppressed in this aspect as well. The Arabs have always been aware of the importance of gifting and give cultural diplomacy prominence in their dealings with other societies.

Let us explore some of the manifestations of exchange between Arab civilisation and other civilisations by means of excerpts from Judge Al-Rashid bin Al-Zubayr's book "Relics and Antiques" from the 5th century AH (11th century CE). This book is considered to be one of the most important books that dealt with the exchange of gifts and precious items throughout the entire Islamic world, from Sindh to Andalusia, starting from the Sassanid era to the Fatimids. It is a rare book that reflects the Arab's appreciation for the idea of exchanging gifts and their deep-rooted culture of generosity and largesse. Ibn Al-Zubayr mentions that the emperor of China wrote the following to Mu'awiyah ibn Abi Sufyan:

> *"From the emperor of properties who is served by the daughters of a thousand kings, whose residence is built with bricks of gold, who keeps a thousand elephants in his stables and who possesses two rivers that water aloes and camphor – the fragrance of which may be smelt 20 miles away, to the emperor of Arabs who worships none but Allah and associates none unto Him. To continue, I have sent you a gift. It is not merely a gift, it is a collector's item. So, send me what your Prophet taught regarding what is permissible and what is forbidden; and dispatch someone who will explain the same to me. Peace."*

The gift was a book containing the secrets of their sciences. It is said that it later became the property of Khalid bin Yazid bin

Mu'awiyah and he would use the knowledge it contained to fashion marvellous works of craftsmanship and other wondrous items.[1]

Exchanges between those in authority and power from different cultures in the Middle Ages took on a special nature, as gifts were a means of introducing cultures and forms of knowledge through the symbolism and connotations they carried in both their form and content. By way of this friendly gift, whether intentionally or unintentionally, the Chinese emperor showcases his peoples' mastery in the crafts of writing and bookbinding in the form of a present; and, likewise, introduces the knowledge of various crafts and industries between the book's pages and from within its content. In return, he asks Mu'awiya ibn Sufyan to introduce him to this monotheistic faith that differs from his own – it is to be expected that, in addition, the teacher whom he requested to be sent will, in turn, teach him the Arabic language and the arts of writing and calligraphy.

Gifting was not limited to those in power and authority, for it became a tradition amongst the scholars, rulers and the general populace in any given society.

A Holistic Acculturation Process

The cultural diplomacy of the Middle Ages took novel and sophisticated forms within what art historians called the "gift economy". In fact, the exchanges that took place within this economy were frequent and developed in all directions, spreading between many different parties until it resulted in what the scholar of art history, Oleg Grabar, termed "the culture of common things". Shared between radically different civilisations, this strongly indicates that difference does not spoil friendship.

---

1   Bin Zubayr, Kitab Al-dhakhai'r wal Tuhaf, ed. Muhammad Hamidullah, Salahuddin Al_Munjid, Da'irat Al matbu'at wal Nashr, Kuwait, 1959, pp9-10

The word "things" in this context refers to artistic artefacts of various genres and tastes on diverse media, ranging from everyday pottery to the finest gemstones and precious raw materials, such as elephant or rhinoceros ivory. These artistic masterpieces, both functional and aesthetic, were transmitted from one people to another through commercial exchanges and before that by way of gifts exchanged by rulers amongst themselves. The function of the gift in the political sphere was essentially diplomatic; and yet they carried in their depths messages, ideas and cultural innuendoes par excellence. Thus, it would be more accurate to say that these artefacts constituted an essential expression of cultural diplomacy throughout the Middle Ages.

We can state, with a large measure of consensus, that the gift economy and the economy of commodities are two symbiotic economies that complete each other; overlapping, or in many cases even dissolving into one another. More accurately, the fundamental difference between a gift and a commodity lies in the origin and source of each. For if a merchant may purchase his goods from one country and sell them in another land, it is supposed that a gift is sourced from the country or culture of the one who is gifting it. Ralph Emerson expresses this in poetic terms: "Rings and jewels are not gifts, but apologies for gifts. The only gift is a portion of thyself. Thou must bleed for me. Therefore, the poet brings his poem; the shepherd, his lamb; the farmer, corn; the diver, coral or pearls; the miner, a stone; the painter, his picture; the girl, a handkerchief of her own sewing. This is right and pleasing, for it restores society in so far to the primary basis, when a man's biography is conveyed in his gift, and every man's wealth is an index of his merit."[1]

---

1   Ralph Waldo Emerson, Emerson's Essays, Dar Al-ahliyyah for publication and distribution, Jordan, first edition, 1999 p256

We should not be surprised that the emperor of China presents a book crafted by his countrymen and awaits a copy of the Qur'an from Mu'awiyah, the khalifah of the Muslims in return.

On the other hand, an amusing Arabic story indicates the decorum required of a person presenting the gift, who is supposedly well-versed in the nature and mores of their counterpart, in order that they may not inadvertently cause offence or bring shame, as is evident from Al-Ma'mun's acknowledgement of Abu Dulf's gift and his fear of offending his womenfolk. It is told that on a festive occasion, Abu Dulf bin 'Isa Al-'Ajli gifted Al-Ma'mun one hundred bales of saffron in silken nets loaded on top of one hundred well-bred, maroon she-asses. The gift arrived whilst Al-Ma'mun was in the company of his womenfolk. It was announced to him: "Al-Qasim bin 'Isa has sent you one hundred loads of saffron on one hundred mules." Al-Ma'mun greatly desired to see how they had been sent to him; yet was loathe to expose his womenfolk to an unbecoming sight. He asked about the beasts of burden – are they male or female? They answered: "Indeed, they are she-asses, all well-bred and not a single male amongst them." Al-Ma'mun was well-pleased by this and replied: "I knew that the man was far wiser than to dispatch any other."

A Gift's Functions: Enhancing Knowledge and Witnessing History

Historical sources mention stories related to gifts that have become famous – and in some cases infamous – for various reasons. To illustrate, we choose the Trojan Horse, the gifts of Bilqis, Queen of Sheba to Sulayman the Wise, and Harun Al-Rashid's gift to the king of France in the Middle Ages. In contemporary language, the Trojan Horse might be described as a "poisoned gift". In essence, a gift is a token of love and affection but in the case of Troy it was a killer trap. The first reference to this appears in Homer's epic, "The Iliad" which is considered to be one of the greatest of Western epic poems. Troy was a rival city and the Greeks tried to capture it by force for 10 years but were unsuccessful because its fortresses and defences were impenetrable. Given that war is deceit, the hero Odysseus decided to resort to deception instead of military force that hitherto had yielded no results. The Greeks pretended to concede defeat and announce their failure in conquering Troy. They then fashioned a huge wooden horse as their gift to the stubborn city in order that they may start a new era of peace and friendship. Troy rejoiced at the news and opened its gates in order to pull the horse into the city. The Trojans arranged major festivities in honour of this precious gift. But the wooden horse was hollow and bore the fiercest of Greek soldiers in its cavity, who infiltrated the city at night, killed its people by surprise, seized it and freed their own captives.

As for Bilqis' gift to King Sulayman, the intention behind it was a test to ascertain whether he was a king or a prophet. In other words, to see whether he was attached to the temporal world and its trappings or to religion and its values. The Christian narrative offers the following text: "And when the queen of Sheba heard of the fame of Solomon, she came to prove Solomon with hard questions at Jerusalem, with a very great company, and camels that bore spices, and gold in abundance, and precious stones: and when she came to Solomon, she communed with him of all that was in her heart."[1]

In the Qur'anic narrative, the following two verses are to be found in Surat Al-Naml:

"34. She said, "When kings enter a city, they devastate it, and subjugate its dignified people. Thus, they always do.

---

1   New International Bible, Old Testament, 1 Kings 10:2

35. "I am sending them a gift and will see what the envoys bring back."

The Christian version provides a list of the gifts given by Bilqis – a camel laden with perfume, gold and precious stones – whereas the Qur'anic narrative differs in that it does not detail the nature of the presents. A few exegetes, including Al-Tabari, mentioned there were pageboys and maids. Thus, Sulayman commanded the boys to perform their ablution from the elbow upwards and the maids from the elbow downwards in order to preserve their modesty.

Regardless of the difference, both the Christian narrative and the Qur'anic story agree that the purpose of sending the gift was to ascertain Sulayman's nature; and to determine whether he was a king seeking the trappings and riches of this world or a prophet seeking to spread the religion. Bilqis will then make her decision according to what she discovers: if the man is a prophet, then she has no power or strength over him, but if he is a king then he will be tempted by the gifts and will be no more regal than her and her kingdom and she will not comply with his request.

In addition to the above, Avionam Shalem, of the University of Munich,[1] points out that adopting the interpretation of gift movement as a methodology allows us to track the methods of transmission of historical information, whether real or fabricated. Gifts and other precious items are viewed as "remnants of the past", special items that act as stimulants for memory and allow certain events to be kept alive in the collective memory in a way that facilitates the perpetuation of a legend or a historical narrative. He finds "the migration of these remnant pieces from one cultural

---

1 Lecture "Objects as carriers of real or contrived memories in a Cross-cultural context: the Case of the Medieval Diplomatic Presents and Trophies" on the 7/11/2003, at a conference in Berlin organized by the Institute of World Cultures, titled "Migrant Images" On the concept of gifting and gits pp101-102

space to another to be incredibly interesting due to the cultural knowledge that they carry".

Harun Al-Rashid and Charlemagne

In this regard, we mention the gift of Caliph Harun Al-Rashid to the Emperor Charlemagne – a gift that combines wit and cultural capital in the same way as we have described before. The Caliph Harun Al-Rashid was a well-known figure in European circles as a result of his diplomatic relations with the Roman Emperor Charlemagne. Various embassies and missives were exchanged between them as mentioned in the royal Carolingian annuals in the period between 806 and 797 CE, where the gifts sent by Harun Al-Rashid – whom the Franks call the king of Persia– are described thus:

"They approached the emperor and presented unto him gifts sent by the king of Persia. A tent, with many-coloured fabrics. Great in stature and superior in beauty. All the fabrics and stays were woven from the best types of linen and dyed with the most brilliant of hues. Likewise, the king of Persia's gift included many garments woven from the finest silk, perfumes, ointments and balsams in addition to a strange and wonderful copper clock. The twelve hands move according to a water clock that houses twelve copper spheres, one of which drops every hour, on the hour emitting a pleasing metallic ring. Likewise, the clock contains twelve figurines of knights atop their steeds who emerge from twelve windows at the closing of each hour, locking the windows that opened before them as they return. This clock includes many other wonders which cannot be described now, as they are so many. In addition to these gifts, the envoys carried two copper candelabras, astonishing in their size and height. All these gifts were dispatched to the Emperor Charlemagne, to his palace in the city of Achen." [1]

---

1   Mansur Abdulhakim, Sayyid Muluk Bani Al-'Abbas Harun Al-Rashid, The Caliph whom History deliberately defamed, Dar Al-Kitab Al-Arabi, Beirut, 2011 p292

In his book on Harun Al-Rashid, Mansur Abdulhakim relates the following anecdote: "The clock stoked the emperor's astonishment as well as that of his entourage, for the monks believed that there must be a demon within that inhabited the clock and moved it. They approached the clock in the dead of night, bringing axes and smashed it only to find nothing but mechanics and its working parts within. Emperor Charlemagne was deeply saddened and summoned an assembly of scientists and skilled craftsmen to try to repair the clock and restart it, but all their attempts to do so failed. Some of his advisors counselled him to write to the Caliph Harun Al-Rashid requesting an Arab team to repair it, but Charlemagne replied: 'I would be deeply ashamed for the king of Baghdad to know that we have committed a disgrace in the name of all of France'."

In the modern era, the gift is considered a major element integral to diplomatic work, as countries allocate budgets specifically for it and assign departments responsible for follow-up and accountability. In democratic countries, official gifts remain the property of the state.

From a financial perspective, the gift constitutes a critically important element in market economies, causing them to become enlivened during public occasions and holidays for all cultures, peoples and nations as well as private celebrations such as marriages, birthdays and joyful occasions in general that represent opportunities for celebration.

Arab Soft Power in the Heart of Europe: The Arab World Institute

The concept of soft power gave permission for – and marked the entry of the whole world into – a new era in what is termed cultural diplomacy, the basis of which is the use of cultural products to influence hearts and minds. The point is to create a collective general, psychological and cultural environment that is based on a homogenous way of thinking and way of living. The world is swiftly moving towards an ever-increasing consolidation of major values, especially freedom, democracy and human rights. It is an intelligent investment in culture and the human resources of other nations which leaves a mark deep in their minds and consciences so that they, in turn, become spreaders of these shared values. Culture is the pathway and entrance to hearts, it is the carrier of ideas, values and beliefs and no weapons are to be found in this field other than the weapons of rational persuasion and psychological impact. It is far better and longer lasting because as an idea spreads, it takes ways and follows paths that do not recognise red lines, boundaries or customs barriers.

Cultural diplomacy's target audience is the citizens of other countries who are called upon, in various forms, to adopt and share perceptions and values. In establishing the Arab World Institute in Paris, we have an important example and model to hand. When I was ambassador in Paris, the Council of Arab Ambassadors was homogenous and included an elite group of ambassadors with experience, expertise and awareness.[1] Culture was a major priority in which they took great interest. We often used to discuss the best way to present our Arab culture in this capital replete with art and thought, in order that it may fulfil its role as a soft power in the service of Franco-Arab relations.

Coincidentally, it just so happened that two successive French governments shared our vision during that period. I lived through the premiership of two presidents of the Fifth Republic, namely

---

1   Including, but not limited to Yusuf Bil Abbas (Dean of Arab ambassadors and the Moroccan Ambassador) Tahir Al-Masri (the Jordanian Ambassador), Al-Hadi Mabruk (the Tunisian Ambassador), 'Isa Al-Hamd (Kuwaiti Ambassador), Hamad Al-Kawari (the Qatari Ambassador), Ibrahim Al-Sus (Palestinain Ambassador), Yusuf Shakur (Syrian Ambassador), Jamil Hujaylan (Saudi Ambassador), Khalifah Al-Mubarak (UAE Ambassador), Ahmad Makki (Omani Ambassador) and other prominent Arab ambassadors.

President Valéry Giscard d'Estaing (1974 – 1981) and President François Mitterrand (1981 – 1996). D'Estaing's Foreign Minister was Jean François-Poncet (1978 – 1981) and Mitterand's Foreign Minister was Claude Cheysson (1981 – 1984). Both of them paid great attention to relations with the Arab world to the extent that Minister Claude Cheysson enacted the good practice of a monthly meeting with Arab ambassadors in one of the famous rest houses outside Paris on weekends. During these weekends, conversations were open-ended, not subject to a set agenda and took place in an atmosphere replete with friendship, even though unforeseen emergencies occasionally imposed themselves. I recollect that we were a group of ambassadors who were aware, by virtue of our personal interests, of the role of culture and its centrality in the dialogue of civilisations and international understanding. It was patently clear to us that the idea others held of the Arab world had become tainted as a result of vagueness and confusion. Thus, we alighted on the idea of introducing Arab culture in a discreet way, far from the short-term fluctuations of current policies.

The idea behind the Arab World Institute came to light during Minister Poncet's tenure and took shape during these aforementioned meetings with Minister Cheysson. In truth, I feel extremely pleased with my humble role throughout – from presenting the idea, during the project phase and the time that the Arab World Institute was established, through to the present time where it has become a fixed reality in the cultural life of Paris.

It is worthy of note that President d'Estaing allocated the land opposite the Hilton Hotel in the 15th arrondissement to be the headquarters of the Arab World Institute in Paris and the Arab ambassadors were enthusiastic about this choice given the prominence and importance of this commercial location.

When President Mitterrand, a man who was passionate about culture and paid great attention to it, succeeded him, he was of the opinion that the allocated land was not suitable due to the fact that it was a commercial area. In fact, he considered that the institution was an institute of a purely cultural nature. Thus, in his estimation, its headquarters should be located in the cultural heart of Paris, near the universities and institutions of the fifth arrondissement.

Today, I admit that this matter initially disturbed some Arab ambassadors who at the time mistakenly believed that Mitterrand was working to diminish the importance of the institute by isolating it from an important commercial centre; and that the socialists did not have the same enthusiasm for Arab-French relations.

Mitterrand made his decision and the land on which the institute is now located was chosen. One of France's greatest architects, Jean Nouvel, was elected to design the institute – who, as fate would have it – would later also be the architect of the distinctive architectural masterpiece that today hosts the National Museum of Qatar in Doha.

With the passage of time, it became clear that Arab-French relations remained excellent during Mitterrand's presidency, to the point that the socialist president's first official trip abroad was to the Kingdom of Saudi Arabia; and this was a strong indication of his keenness to maintain cordial relations.

Mitterrand's choice was proven correct, and it became clear that his decision to allocate the site in the cultural centre of Paris was a far-sighted, informed one. The institute evolved into an effective beacon, the epicentre for activities in the service of Arab culture in one of the largest cultural capitals in the world – right in the heart of Paris.

The Arab World Institute is a cultural bridge between the Arab Levant and Maghreb on the one hand and the West on the other. It is the fruit of a partnership between France and all the member countries in the Arab League. From a legal standpoint, the institute is an establishment subject to French civic law. It calls for the introduction of French and European audiences to the Arab world's contributions to global civilisations, in addition to encouraging dialogue between East and West.

The Arab World Institute's promotional literature states that it seeks to encourage studies about and deepen knowledge of the Arab world in France, its language, civilisation and efforts with regard to development. The institute also strives to support cultural exchanges, communication and co-operation between France and all Arab countries, especially in the fields of science and technology. It contributes proactively towards the nurturing relationships between France and the Arab world, which in turn strengthens links between the Arab world and Europe in general. Directly after the institute's inauguration in 1987, it speedily became a distinguished space that was automatically integrated into the cultural fabric of the French capital. The institute included a museum of Arab-Islamic art and a specialist library, as well as a lecture hall. Year after year, it succeeded in hosting and presenting a variety of diverse events covering artistic, intellectual and cultural fields of the Arab world including music, cinematic arts, dance, fine arts, sculpture, architecture, photography, youth programmes and many others. It also flung its doors wide open, warmly welcoming debates, dialogue, and intellectual exchanges by means of seminars, lectures and symposia in addition to its quarterly magazine, "Qantarah" (The Arch).

In all honesty, the institute could have been far larger, and its impact felt far more widely, had it received the requisite Arab response! Right from the start, it was noted that some Arab countries were often lax and delayed greatly in submitting their contributions in a timely manner, which had a directly negative impact on the institute's financial situation and weakened the Arab countries' status when it came to forming and implementing policies or influencing them appropriately.

The power of culture in our time has taken on a new form, based on persuasion and temptation, facilitated by the ability of culture, ideas, scientific production and its technological applications to facilitate communication between people in an informal way that leaves its mark in the new perceptions it instils about the Other.

In addition, dialogue and discussion draw out the dreams of the world's citizens and harness them to paint a snapshot of shared humanity that all may participate in.

Principles of Cultural Diplomacy

The basic model of cultural diplomacy consists of four constants: addressing the 'other' according to the protocols of foreign policy and relying on indirect influence by causing the counterpart to care about the culture that is being promoted. The 'other' should neither be a state nor an official institution, but rather individuals hailing from various fields within civil society. The results to be achieved should be relatively long term and none would be short term. In his introduction to a series of lectures he delivered in New York, the French cultural advisor Antonin Baudry[1] said: "The goals of cultural diplomacy are not cultural, but rather belong to foreign policy that relies on education, research and culture as a means to achieve its goals. Despite this, despatching an ambassador means acknowledging a power and establishing a state-to-state relationship, whereas establishing cultural diplomacy assumes recognition of the intellectual system behind the power itself, as well as the organisation of an intersocietal relationship. Its goal, or game, is to create relationships between the two powers based on a coalition of interests instead of those involving pressure and hegemony."

Baudry believes that the path to activating cultural diplomacy is embodied in a process of transformation that is built on three

---

[1] Antonin Baudry, the French cultural advisor to the United States, presented a positive series of lectures on cultural diplomacy entitled: The Power of the Other – why does cultural diplomacy work? This diplomat has a cheerful disposition and a keen sense of humor, who penned a graphic novel "Quai d'Orsay" under his pseudonym Abel Lanzac, winning the prize for the best album at the Angoulême International Comics Festival in 2013. His lectures can be heard on this link: http://savoirs.ens.fr/expose.php?id=650 (accessed 6/11/2014)

mechanisms: persuasion, temptation and education. And if we recall that the relationship is an intersocietal one, then both elements of persuasion and temptation will be directed towards elements of civic society and not institutions alone. Persuasion and temptation are intensively utilised in all artistic products that convey a cultural message by relying on aesthetics, as is the case with literature and the arts, including cinema. In fact, it often happens that an institution directly opposes the work of cultural diplomacy through its political edicts as happened during the Cold War, for example, in the case of the Soviet ambassador who did not obtain the approval of his country's authorities to distribute famous Soviet film tapes such as Eisenstein's film "Battleship Potemkin", the Vasilyev brothers' "Chapayev" and Pudovkin's film adapted from Maxim Gorky's famous novel "Mother".[1] In order to enable the masses to have access to these films and to be able to watch them, the ambassador deliberately left the door of the film store in his residence open, to facilitate their theft and subsequent screening to people. This incident is told by the French political activist and director, René Vautier, who in 1950 directed the film "Afrique 50", the first French anti-colonial film short. The film remained banned for 40 years; and Vautier was imprisoned for a year because of it.[2]

History reveals that persuasion and temptation may have a deeper impact than force and coercion, which is actually what took place

---

[1] The Battleship Potemkin, or The Destroyer Potemkin is a silent film with Russian subtitles by director Sergei Eisenstein, produced in 1926. It deals with the Russian Revolution of 1905 and is considered one of the most important films in the history of world cinema. "Chapayev", directed by the Vasliyev Brothers is a Soviet film produced in 1934. It is the story of Red Army commander Vasily Ivanovich Chapayev (1887 – 1919), who is considered to be one of the heroes of the Russian Civil War. As for the film "Mother", which dates back to the yeat 1926, it is an adaptation of the novel by Maxim Gorky (1868 – 1936) which he wrote in 1906. Gorky is considered to be the founding father of the socialist realist literary school.

[2] Antonin Baudry mentioned it in his first lecture entitled "The Power of the Other, why Cultural Diplomacy works"

between the Greek and Roman civilisations. The Latin poet Horace says: "After its invasion at the hands of Roman soldiers, Greece, in turn, vanquished the heart of its fierce conqueror by carrying arts and literature deep into the heart of the rural Roman countryside."[1] This phrase became famous and was used as a renowned saying to describe Greece's cultural victory, which surpassed Rome's military victory. Although the Roman armies brought bloody conflict with all the ferocity that warriors could muster to Greece, Greece in turn carried the fine arts in their many forms including theatre, poetry, architecture and philosophy into the Roman settlements and encampments which, during that era, were no more than simple villages. If military victories shape political geographies for a limited period, then cultural victories shape human thought and their prevailing mentality for far longer, as well as influencing behaviours and beliefs.

If we recall, for example, those beautiful, picturesque scenes that concluded the Beijing Olympic Games in 2008, we become further convinced that this concept of soft power is directly related to the cultural image that it portrays of this civilisation or that. For China presented to the world an image of Chinese magnificence that combined the ancient past of one of the greatest civilisations in history alongside a present that is sweeping the entire world with its technology, investments and commodities.

It was not the show itself that sent a bolt of amazement through me, as here I am not talking about the constituent factors of Chinese economic power, being as they are only one of the prominent aspects of this country's present-day profile. China has done its best to restore its archaeological monuments, value its huge material heritage and include it as a UNESCO World Heritage Site. But

---

1   Graeia capta ferum victorem cepit et artes Intulit agrestic Latio: La Grece conquise a conquis son farouche vainqueur; elle a fait reigner l'art dans l'agreste Latium.
    Beule CE (1865) Revue de Deux Mondes T. 56 p 312

what concerns me most here is China's efforts in developing its film industry, similar to North Korea and Japan in particular, in the context of promoting an image of China that exudes beauty and joy. I do not separate this strategy of the world of images (ie film-making) from the entryism of a number of Chinese writers and authors who write novels and short stories that compete with the pantheon of immortals in the world of the Nobel Prize for Literature. Neither would I separate it from the efforts of many Chinese cultural organisations - first and foremost amongst them being the Confucius Institute – in spreading Chinese culture, complete with its language, arts, music and calligraphy supported by subsidies that are offered to help nurture this in many different places all over the world.

China and its foreign cultural policy are a perfect example of the interdependence of factors influencing economic power and the inseparability of politics and culture in shaping effective soft power.

Indeed, I look towards what my own country has achieved in the cultural arena during its hosting of the FIFA Football World Cup in 2022. For this is not merely a sporting event, it has outgrown this definition and is a festival of heritage couched in cultural diplomacy that has a meaningful impact on embedding impressions of countries, societies and civilisation in attendees' minds. Qatar, undoubtedly, was fully aware of the importance of this wager and its constructive role.

We may also speak of other experiments taken from France's forays into the field of political diplomacy, from its cultural activities, its films, its radio stations (Monte Carlo's broadcast in the Arabic language, for example) and its television channels (eg TV 5 and France 25), not to mention the French way of life as presented in the sophisticated French banquet and its historic traditions as well as the marketing of Paris as the capital of arts, lights and culture. So much so that it embraced the Arab culture to which I belong by welcoming the Arab World Institute. The moral background and conclusion of these comments is that every form of soft power and diplomacy strives towards spreading culture.

Selected Means of Cultural Diplomacy

Regardless of the relationship between cultural diplomacy, public diplomacy and cultural exchange, we are faced with interconnected concepts, given that cultural diplomacy, at its core, does not deviate from the establishment of international relations via the channels of culture, arts, science and education. These are relationships that are intended to be developed and are entrusted with goals and objectives that are expressed in diplomatic language by the term, or concept of "mutual understanding". Political scientist Milton Cummings defines cultural diplomacy as "the exchange of ideas, information, values, systems, traditions, beliefs and other aspects of culture with the aim of promoting mutual understanding".

However, this general perception requires an effort to present a model lifestyle and a system of values. Every nation has the right to disseminate the essence of its heritage, its culture and its character. It is clear that cultural diplomacy is based on cultural co-operation between sovereign states, recognised political entities, ministries representing various governments and cultural policies. This means that, via official relations between countries, the doors are open for them to introduce the culture of this people or that and for the cross-fertilisation of perceptions, ideas, symbols and artistic creations. On the other hand, it is a cultural policy that joins governments and nations together for the sake of "mutual understanding", that is, building a common symbolic, intellectual and artistic space in which to enrich the self as well as the other and to build a creative dialectic between different cultures.

Some countries that distinguished themselves in the field of cultural diplomacy established state institutions, bodies and structures of an international nature, varying in strength and influence. Amongst these is the phenomenal resources that L'Organisation Internationale de la Francophonie provides for the dissemination of the cultures of the countries with which it is affiliated. There are also independent governmental or civil bodies with enormous resources and capabilities in addition to precisely targeted, intelligent programmes used in cultural diplomacy. This is evident and comes prominently to the fore in their work to establish connections with intellectual elites in other countries and their efforts to encourage cultural and academic missions and trips. It is, today, an established and undeniable reality that personal relationships are the basis for building global networks and strong centres of influence on segments of public opinion.

It is known that France used to lead the field in establishing cultural organisations abroad in order to enhance its image overseas, as in 1883 when it created the organisation Alliance Française, a step which Italy then followed six years later by creating the Dante Alighieri, followed by Britain which established the British Council in 1934. These bodies, which took on an independent, non-governmental character, shared common goals, which were mainly the dissemination of language and culture throughout the world and the introduction of the lifestyle of this or that country as well as their cultural, intellectual and artistic products. Naturally, the intention behind this is to create a favourable perception of these countries in the view of the 'other'.

Although we are not in the business of showcasing the history of these organisations that are hugely impactful in the field of cultural diplomacy, we should also not forget what other major organisations do in this same vein. Here we can mention, for example, the German Academic Exchange Service and the German Goethe Institute, which, likewise, aim to encourage the teaching of German language and facilitate academic and scientific activities in Germany. Similar to this is the American Fulbright Program, which has been in operation since the mid-20th century and aims to develop culture, literature, arts and the sciences by means of academic exchanges.

In this regard, we should not lose sight of South Korea's efforts in spreading its language, dramatic, cinematic and musical production and harnessing them as attractive tools by which they can win the hearts of young people around the world.

These different bodies and the examples that we have listed confirm that they are institutions that embody an aspect of soft power that is not necessarily linked to government policies. But the countries' efforts and their public diplomacy combine with the efforts of these non-governmental organisations, regardless of whether they are state-sponsored, such as the British Council, or through private initiatives and funding, such as the Fulbright Program, and will inevitably meet in the tasks assigned to it. Whether these tasks involve increasing the number of language speakers such as in Germany, or promoting culture such as in France, or relying on education as the basis for building human perceptions, such as the British Council, they are in fact all a snapshot of the intersections between culture, politics and diplomatic work.

To return to what we mentioned at the start of this section regarding cultural diplomacy being, in essence, the establishment of international relations through culture, arts, science and education, it is worth reaffirming one of the most important carriers in human history that transmitted the culture, arts and science of one people to another people – the gift.

Despite these contemporary paths of cultural diplomacy, I want to draw attention to the fact that these deep meanings were not merely limited to this era, but existed also in previous eras, as was demonstrated in the phenomenon of presents. I would like to add here that Arabs' interest in and care for individuals who would be responsible for enacting the policies of cultural diplomacy is considered to be an important element leading to its success throughout their history. This is a matter that Yahya Al-Ghazal Al-Jiyani was famous for, as he possessed characteristics that made him well-qualified for this role. The Egyptian historian Abdullah Enan cites this, saying: "A famous example during the rule of Ibn Hisham Al-Umawiyy in Andalusia is Yahya Al-Ghazal Al-Jiyani, who was nicknamed Al-Ghazal (the Gazelle) for his beauty, pleasantness and elegance. He was a prolific published poet who excelled in writing love poetry and has many sophisticated verses in the praise of women. Above all this, he was a scholar who specialised in philosophy and astronomy. He had penned an 'urjuza (a didactic poem, using the rajaz meter) detailing the various sciences that unfortunately did not reach us. He often criticised jurists and would campaign against them until he earned their fury and they accused him of heresy as a result of his outspokenness and free thinking. Moreover, Al-Ghazal became famed for the integrity of his thought, admirable planning, tact and cunning. These qualities made him well-qualified to undertake dangerous diplomatic missions later during the rule of Abdulrahman bin Hakam".[1]

It is noteworthy that bin Hakam sent Yahya Al-Ghazal to Constantinople, along with Yahya ibn Habib, with a letter and a gift to the emperor, who received them warmly. From then on, Andalusia became the centre of diplomacy in the Islamic world at a time when the Abbasid state was suffering from dissolution. Cordoba turned into a destination for Christian states, led by Constantinople which, until the eighth century, was the centre of its diplomacy. During the reign of Al-Nasir li-Din Allah (d.961 CE), Cordoba experienced diplomatic activity with the Christian West the like of which it had never seen before. Treaties, embassies, correspondence and diplomatic relations all became active between Cordoba and the majority of Christian states.

---

1   Muhammad Abdullah 'Anan The Islamic State in Al-Andalus, vol. 1 Maktabat AlKhanji, Cairo, fourth edition, 1997, p 253

Narrations relate that envoys of Emperor Constantine the Seventh, Constantinople's Caesar, also known as Porphyrogenitus, were dispatched with precious gifts to Al-Nasir in 948 CE. The Andalusian story conveys many intriguing details about these envoys that shed light on diplomatic protocols of that age, for it tells us that Al-Nasir sent his messengers to receive the Byzantine envoys upon their arrival to the shore in order to assist and guide them. When they drew close to Cordoba, he sent some of his troops to celebrate their arrival, then he sent the two youths Yasir and Tamam, who accompanied them, to the guest quarters in the palace of the crown prince, on the outskirts of Cordoba. They were prevented from meeting both the elite and the commoners and he arranged for a group of palace staff and soldiers to be at their service. On the 11th day of Rabi' al-Awwal in that self-same year, Al-Nasir left the Palace of Al-Zahra' and went out towards the Palace of Cordoba in order to receive them and sat in the resplendent majlis. It was a memorable day in Andalusia."[1]

Culture and the Rainbow of Diplomacy

Before I was entrusted with the task of managing cultural affairs in the State of Qatar, I was fortunate to find myself delving into the world of diplomacy in globally renowned epicentres such as Paris and New York. However, as I was learning the ropes and striving to perform the tasks assigned to me, I could not shake an overwhelming feeling that gave expression to something I was slowly discovering within the diplomatic community: what are the shared commonalities that we can build on? How do we reduce the distances caused by differences in political goals and interests, whilst growing the space for coalition? This was my aim between local

---

1   Op. cit. p 452

and global, between the utilitarian and the humanitarian: how can we be here and there at the same time?

I was, and still am – perhaps like many other diplomats – obsessed with the difficult art of building relationships, which requires one to constantly look at the half-full section of the glass. This is not out of alleged optimism, but rather out of necessity. For what is diplomacy if not the art of meeting, understanding and shared construction?

Not to mention that the most enjoyable opportunities that are granted a diplomat are what is termed multilateral diplomacy. Fortunately, I was my country's permanent representative to the UN, and before that to UNESCO, so I saw, observed and truly lived through the experience of what collective diplomatic work means.

Despite the divergence in interests, the multiplicity of specialisations and participating parties requires that each party approach the matter with a positive spirit – intentions have no place at the table here! The very nature of this work makes each party dependent on the other, given that in the end, the vote will be secret. In this regard, there is absolutely no room whatsoever for the imposition of opinions, regardless of the strength and calculations of each person. This means, as a matter of necessity, relying on rational arguments and the efficiency of persuasion to convince everyone; or at least the majority of those who will participate in the vote. This is the field of creative diplomacy par excellence.

In fact, one of the advantages of this multilateral diplomacy is its reliance on the mentality of human convergence. Every nation's representative knows their counterparts well on a personal level. So, teamwork or collective work becomes like a strange mixture of state interests, regional cliques, personal relationships, similar inclinations, convergences, rational thinking and the search for the common good.

Today, we live in an era in which culture flourishes only within a cohesive, integrated system of human development, and every imbalance in this system inevitably leads to placing culture at the lowest rung of the ladder due to the lack of necessary conditions for cultural creativity.

The Direction of the Compass

Shortly after World War II, humanity demonstrated clear indications that it had begun to learn and internalise its bitter lesson once the United Nations was established. The founding of this organisation was a major event and a clear declaration that collective rationality requires the debate to be managed with all its difficulties and obstacles, instead of indulging in unbecoming barbarism that no longer befits the intelligence at which the human race has arrived.

The direction of the compass had to be changed.

Perhaps UNESCO, with its focus on culture, science and education, was the most prominent element in this new agenda set on transforming the world. The goal of this transformation was to write the chapters of a new history based on a set of principles, ideas and ethics that express the essence of nations' dreams.

This is what made UNESCO a departure from the crucible of local and national cultures and launched it into a far more expansive horizon – global culture. It could not possibly have achieved this except by gradually transforming the collective mindset in order to consider what is relevant to common humanity and to the universe at large. It is, indeed, a forum for dialogue on the future of humanity. In this sense, UNESCO was, and still is, based on multilateral diplomacy that is aimed at building a common future in which science, education, and culture all play a proactive role in strengthening the underpinnings and solid infrastructure for this highly desired transformation.

The truth is that the change in the compass' direction, despite the heaving waves, was not merely a declaration of intent, despite the fact that change required many resources, the most prominent of which was finances.

On the new global cultural diplomacy

It must be noted that the presence of non-governmental organisations and civil society in relation to cultural diplomacy is not new, even in the field of bilateral diplomacy. Even though its role grew and became more significant as cultural diplomacy developed, changing its forms and diversifying its strategies, it was always an influential component. It is part of a local and global trend which is partially linked to the balances between "political society" and "civil society" in each democratic country whose political system melds its constituent parts together.

Scholars have noted that the political shift in cultural diplomacy occurred after World War I. However, most aspects of this diplomacy were carried out by individuals or groups who were artists, inventors, travellers, mediators or even conquerors. Most of them were not government actors; and this is what makes this free exchange of information and transmission of different cultural perceptions closer to pre-cultural diplomacy in the full sense of the word.[1] It is clear that the absence of official channels, premeditated cultural strategies and the lack of clarity with regard to goals makes this an effort of individuals.

But as soon as state interests and their diplomacy necessitated the presence of cultural diplomacy in its modern institutional sense, the relationship between government work and independent civic cultural organisations diversified. Although the British Council, for example, is an independent body, it works in close collaboration

---

1 See the following research on Cultural Diplomacy: Jessica C. E. Gienow-Hecht and Mark C. Donfried, Searching for a Cultural Diplomacy Berghahn Books, New York, Oxford 2010

with the British government which determines the countries it should be active in. Likewise, the federal government in Germany directs cultural policy and provides financial resources in co-operation with independent entities such as the Goethe-Institut. Accordingly, the work of these non-governmental organisations and independent bodies complements the work of their governments.[1]

This trend, linked to state policies, has given rise to certain opinions that believe cultural diplomacy must be entirely independent of governments and that government entities should not participate in it at all. At its heart, it is a cultural exchange with the outside world in the name of the nation and the people. The people themselves must address their counterparts in the intended countries and define their own goals and set their own activities. This position is more of a reaction to government agencies' monopolisation of the mechanisms of cultural exchange and its goals. On the other hand, however, it has created a kind of suspicion in governments towards non-governmental organisations and civil society in general, because in addition to the difficulties involved in monitoring and directing NGOs, the interests of these organisations may not be entirely congruent with those of the governments they are associated with.

Unlike any other field, it is impossible for any nation to make meaningful offerings in the field of cultural diplomacy without the strong support of non-governmental players active in the creation of culture – whether they be teachers, lecturer, students, artists or inventors[2] – regardless of the fact that their goals may differ, whether slightly or greatly, from those of official government agencies.

In all cases, civil society and its non-governmental organisations are highly efficient at establishing lasting, solid relationships built

---

1   Op. cit.
2   Op. cit.

on dialogue, understanding and mutual trust with individuals and groups in other societies.

Furthermore, non-governmental organisations are able to win the trust of their target audience far more easily and permanently because the traditional patterns of cultural diplomacy hitherto provided by governments have begun to raise questions about their legitimacy and neutrality. People have strong intuition and demand nothing from any form of cultural outreach other than mutual respect in order that the desired state of harmony may be reached.

Thus, UNESCO's experience in multilateral cultural diplomacy provides an important lesson for bilateral cultural diplomacy. There is no escaping interaction between governments and civil society with its NGOs and independent organisations. Nor is it possible to avoid the creation of real partnerships between them and the corporations and individuals providing funding in order to achieve the goals outlined in partnership programmes, cultural exchange or any other initiative directed towards a foreign audience. [1]

We see no contradiction between the two paths of cultural diplomacy, bilateral and multilateral. Both still play an active role in supporting intercultural dialogue and drawing nations closer together, as long as they operate on the basis of respect for diversity and multiplicity, have a willingness to engage in cross-cultural dialogue and interaction, have a commitment to the values of freedom and human rights, and uphold moral and social values.

Cultural Diplomacy and Sports Wagers

For as long as I have busied myself with cultural diplomacy, I have been convinced of its effective role in serving world peace, spreading a culture of respect for the Other, promoting cultural diversity, and having an ability to come up trumps when reinforcing

---

1   Op. cit. pp2 4-25

and promoting ideals. I am conscious of the strong bond between cultural diplomacy and sport in a world in which change has become markedly accelerated, and the world needs to utilise all means of cultural diplomacy at its disposal in order that humanity may enjoy the positive state of coexistence it strives to achieve.

It may cross some people's minds that the field of cultural diplomacy is entirely unrelated to sport; and that sport has far more in common with entertainment than it has with effective diplomatic strategies. However, today we have come to talk of "sports diplomacy" too and this is undoubtedly a branch of cultural diplomacy, for sport is not merely an activity that players and athletes undertake, it is an expansive space and welcoming arena that activates and nurtures international diplomatic relations. Many sports have, over the ages, proven that they are not merely a physical activity undertaken by the body, but a powerful social force and cultural connector. That is why it occupies an important position in social structures to the extent that it is a civilisational marker of many societies.

When I see the progress achieved by my beloved country, Qatar, I see that sport enjoys the same lofty position and advanced status that so many other sectors in our society do. This would not have been possible without the vision of our leadership, which correctly identified it as one of the key components in building up both the individual and the society alike. Our respected leaders strove to activate this vision firstly by planning and providing the necessary infrastructure, then emphasising its importance in the shared consciousness of public opinion. It continued to highlight the need for awareness, the importance of personal health, the role sport plays in simultaneously strengthening social bonds, strengthening mental resilience and strengthening physical immunity until sport became an integral part of contemporary Qatari society today. This is greatly enhanced by devoting one day entirely to an annual celebration of sport – National Sports Day – where all members of the society can celebrate and participate in an environment that is noted for its refined principles and social mores.

Qatar's successful bid to host the 2022 FIFA World Cup™ was one of the fruits of this vision for sport, its role in striving towards achieving world peace, drawing nations closer together, creating understanding between them all and strengthening the bonds between them. Winning the right to host this global tournament was nothing but powerful affirmation of the world's confidence in Qatar and a statement of appreciation for all the efforts invested into the sports sector over the years. Here we are today, having held a hugely successful World Cup and we have earned the world's admiration by fulfilling and honouring all our commitments. The event was distinguished on all levels, and this momentous achievement coincided serendipitously with the major strides we have taken in consolidating our image on the world stage as advocates for world peace and respecters of world cultures in all their creative diversity, simply because sport supports and elevates this message.

We believe that sport has many advantages and that as an integral part of cultural diplomacy, it contributes quickly to rapprochement between nations and peoples due to its extensive spread throughout the world and the high levels of interest it commands amongst the youth demographic. This imbues it with great influential power which may sometimes exceed the impact that traditional diplomatic channels may hope to achieve. We have, on more than one occasion, stressed the strategic role played by cultural diplomacy in bringing peace between nations due to the ability of culture to change a nation's adherence to previously held 'truths'. We are certain that sport plays this role too; and assists greatly in disseminating it everywhere. That is why the more we imbue sports with cultural messages that exhort people to adhere to principled human values, the more we succeed in reducing the scope of conflicts and disagreements amongst humankind.

Sport has contributed to diffusing conflicts between countries and solving problems. It has opened the doors to international meetings and, by virtue of its capacity to be a vehicle for delivering apolitical moral messages, it has succeeded in achieving a key aspect of cultural diplomacy and has been more efficient than formal diplomacy in many cases. We should remember that famous table tennis match that drew together the United States of America and the People's Republic of China and paved the way for a thawing of relations between the two countries. Despite winning the match, the Chinese team managed to avoid humiliating their competitors or lessen their sporting rank. Similarly, the ice hockey match between the United States and the Soviet Union in the 1980 Winter Olympics proved that sporting events are capable of easing the tension in international relations between countries.

My impression of global reality has convinced me of the importance of sport in enhancing world peace. Just as it was essential to revisit the role of culture in international relations, the time has now come to realise the potent effect that sport plays in solidifying these relations. Diplomacy alone is insufficient to solve the differences between nations; peace is not only discussed whilst seated around a negotiating table, and traditional diplomatic work is not entirely successful when it is bereft of a cultural diplomacy that takes into account all its elements, including that of sport. Given that international relations urgently, constantly, need to establish a cultural view between people in order to encourage mutual acquaintance and rapprochement, so sport can be a vessel for this as it is fully capable of achieving the principle of mutual respect and expanding the scope for love. Despite the fact many sports rely on the element of competitiveness as one of their aspects, competitions are all subject to a noble moral charter that demands the acceptance of difference, for the only real constant winner in all competitions is the spirit of sportsmanship that has harnessed these activities as a means of nurturing friendship between nations.

Many politicians have realised the essential role that sport plays in establishing peace, that peace that emanates from within and shines all around. It reminds us of what Nelson Mandela achieved when he used sport as a way to combat racism and wear down hatred between blacks and whites. As we do so, we extrapolate and project the impact that sport can have in bringing people together today, for the same sport that establishes tolerance on the playing fields and amongst the crowds of spectators is also the sport that can lead to tolerance between the nations of the world and encourage international friendships, despite differences. Any nation's individual identity cannot develop except by being open and accepting the other. We should not forget that if we wish to spread tolerance, we must first embed a culture of tolerance in ourselves, and this is a majorly sporting principle.

A consensus exists around the capacity of sport to be a catalyst for nations to know one another, because everyone with an interest in sport finds themselves unthinkingly attached to a connection, bearing in mind that cultural diplomacy is, at its core, connections. Interest in sport introduces cultures to one another, broadens their mutual horizons and provides channels for the exchange of literature, arts, general knowledge and the like. The spectators who follow matches in any sport carry slogans, songs, anthems, mascots, cultural symbols and so much more. Thus, their cultural diversity is presented as they display their heritage in a way that many mistakenly perceive as narrow. However, it comes into its own as it spreads and grows, for when culture diffuses into the atmosphere, it becomes part of the air that everyone breathes.

In cooperation with the Ministry of Culture in Qatar (formerly the Ministry of Culture and Sports), the Supreme Committee for Delivery & Legacy launched a pioneering project whose flagship was a multi-use sports stadium in Rwanda. I visited the project at its start. I met children and young people and told them: "This stadium is for you, a gift from the children of Qatar." My happiness was indescribable when I saw the joy in their eyes. This project was an example of both cultural and sports diplomacy.

Football goes well beyond being a spectator sport that is loved by both young and old. It has an influence on the economy – it provides employment for vast numbers of people. It has an educational influence on society – it teaches young people the importance of ethical sportsmanship and principles, to accept both victory and loss, for today's winner could well be tomorrow's loser. Similarly, it instils in them the value of hard work and sacrifice, because without love for the sport, constant hard work and determination, victory can never be achieved. Football, in particular, is a team game, because goals are scored as a result of intelligent strategy that can only succeed if every team member plays their part correctly.

Sport, generally, is a means of communication between the young and different cultures and this communication is built on mutual respect, peaceful tolerance and shared work in order that ethical principles might live on.

When the State of Qatar put its name forward to take responsibility for hosting the 2022 World Cup™, it was well aware of all these contexts and worked hard to make people's experience of the tournament the best ever. This was an assignment in the field of sports diplomacy that was clear in our minds from the very start.

Chapter Five
The Civilisation of Cultural Dialogue

Dialogue between cultures is not an unusual matter in human civilisation, neither is it a characteristic unique to our current era. Its strands have always been prevalent throughout every era of our history, shifting around according to the ebbs and flows of international relations. By strands, we mean those related to exchange and cooperation between peoples, as the broad meaning of dialogue is well served by these definitions.

If the term "dialogues" is used in Arabic or Greek in the sense of "conversation", it also has connotations of debate, in which two or more people participate for the purpose of rapprochement and understanding. This is the original principle and ethical intent behind every dialogue between both people and cultures, but the patterns of dialogue between cultures diversified and became heterogeneous through history, as they have been governed by fluctuating international relations and evolving forms of technological communication. This term became closely associated with the Greeks, indicating the shared thought process that takes place between two speakers, including what we know about the dialogues of Plato and Socrates. Plato adopted a dialogue method that relies on clarification of an idea and making it easy to present. One of the most famous dialogues is that of "Plato's Banquet" in which he explains how to achieve truth by way of love. Dialogue, according to the Western reference, is based on the meaning of achieving understanding without seeking to convince or vanquish your opponent or achieve a preconceived conclusion. Instead, it is an attempt to exchange opinions between one person and another with the aim of attaining communication on an intellectual level.

Indeed, the Arab Islamic culture has never abandoned dialogue even for a day, as it is the lifeblood of the creative environment in various fields. Dialogue is deeply rooted in its being not merely with reference to Greek heritage, but also because it is built solidly on Qur'anic foundations.

The term "hiwar" (dialogue, conversation) appears in the Qur'an three times – twice in Surat Al-Kahf during the narration of the owner of two gardens when he speaks with a friend who does not possess much money. Allah, Most High, mentions them in the first instance saying: "And he had fruit, so he said to his companion while he was conversing with him: "I am greater than you in wealth and mightier in [numbers of] men." (Al-Kahf: 34). He also mentions them again in the same chapter: "His companion said to him whilst they were talking: "Have you disbelieved in He who created you from dust, then from a drop of sperm, then proportioned you [perfectly as] a human?" (Al-Kahf: 37). As for the third verse, it occurs in Surat Al-Mujadilah, in the words of Allah The Most High: "Certainly Allah has heard the speech of the one who argues with you, [O Muhammad], concerning her husband and directs her complaint to Allah. And Allah hears your dialogue; indeed, Allah is All-Hearing, All-Seeing." (Al-Mujadilah: 1).

By this, the Noble Qur'an granted dialogue a lofty status, calling for it to be adopted as a medium for communication and understanding: "Invite to the way of your Lord with wisdom and good instruction; and dialogue with them in a way that is best. Indeed, your Lord is Most Knowing of who have strayed from His way and He is Most Knowing of who is [rightly] guided." (Al-Nahl: 125). The levels of dialogue and the entities involved were many, as the Noble Qur'an speaks to polytheists as well as with People of the Book – Jews and Christians –and conveys to us scenes of the dialogues that take place between the prophets and their nations. It demonstrates to us the ideal image of what dialogue means, or looks like – for example, the scenes of dialogue between Allah The Exalted, the Angels and Satan. From this, Allah The Almighty's saying: ""Remember when your Lord said to the Angels, 'I am going to place a successive [human] authority on earth." They asked Allah: "Will You place in it someone who will spread corruption there and shed blood while we glorify Your praises and proclaim Your holiness?" Allah responded: "I know what you do not know." (Al-Baqarah : 30) Other examples include Allah's dialogue with the prophets, may peace be upon them, an example of this being His conversation with Musa (Moses), peace be upon him: "When Moses came at the appointed time and his Lord spoke to him, he asked: "My Lord! Reveal Yourself to me so I may see You." Allah answered: "You cannot see Me! But look at the mountain. If it remains firm in its place, only then will you see Me." When his Lord appeared to the mountain, He levelled it to dust and Moses collapsed unconscious. When he recovered, he cried: "Glory be to You! I turn to You in repentance and I am the first of the believers." (Al-Araf : 143)

Arab Islamic civilisation is based on this dialogic reference, to the extent that it seems to me that dialogue is closer to humans' natural disposition. That is why I appreciate Taha 'Abdulrahman's statement: "The origin of speech is dialogue, for the truth of the words that the first man spoke was a dialogic truth, and this dialogue was intrinsically connected to nature, entwined with nature and inextricably connected to the spirit; only later were specific refinements and controls introduced into the idea of dialogue".[1]

---

1 Taha Abdulrahman Alhiwar ufuqan lil-fikr, The Arab Network for Research and Publication, 2013 p28

This means that dialogue is inherent in humans. More so, it means that humans can be defined as dialogic creatures, for their "civilisational dimension" - to borrow a phrase from Ibn Khaldun – recognises the need for dialogue with others, as no man is an island. A person cannot live alone, therefore his social dimension, ie his civilisational aspect, makes it imperative that they talk to their fellow human(s). This perception of dialogue was also profoundly reflected in Islamic jurisprudence, exemplified in Imam Al-Shafi'i's saying: "My opinion is correct, yet may be wrong and someone else's opinion is wrong, yet may be correct." This is a golden rule in the culture of dialogue that guided generations, as it gave them the opportunity to understand the foundations of dialogue based on respecting the other's opinion rather than overcoming it. Another elegant example that I unearthed is Imam Malik bin Anas' response when the Caliph Al-Mansur decided to force everyone to follow Imam Malik's book "Al-Muwatta'", as it was (and remains) the foremost text in fiqh and hadith (jurisprudence and prophetic tradition). Imam Malik refused to have it distributed and insisted: "Let the people be, leave them to choose; each to their own."

Dialogue in the Majilis

The Arabs recognised the importance of dialogue in the creation of knowledge – knowing oneself and knowing the other. Majilis (social, communal gatherings and councils) were held amongst Muslims, between Muslims and the People of the Book; and even between Muslims and Magians (Zoroastrians). These gatherings were not restricted to intellectuals or those concerned with the sciences, they also concerned the rulers. Abu Hayyan Al-Tawhidi tells us of events that occur in these majilis in his book and the most important debates that were widespread during his time. He divided them into 37 nights and, in them, recounted what took place between him and the opposing minister, Bani Buwayh, whose majlis was an intellectual, literary and cultural forum. Amongst the most famed of Al-Tawhidi's reports is the debate between logic and grammar which took place between Matta ibn Yunus and Abu Sa'id Al-Serafy as he recounts in "Al-Muqtabisat" and "Al-Imta' wa Mu'anasa", including the debates between arithmetic and rhetoric, prose and poetry and many others.

Thus, a debate is a dialogue between two sides on a specific topic in which two opposing opinions are presented. Each then is given the opportunity to make their case. In the history of Arab culture, it is a special element. We find it permeating through books of jurisprudence, literature and history. Ibn Khaldun defined it by saying: "Since the doors of refutation and acceptance in debate are wide and spacious, each debater gives free rein when reasoning and answering — some of which is right; and some of which is wrong. So, the imams needed to establish etiquette and rules, the limits of which the two debaters should observe during their refutation and acceptance. How, for example, should the proposer and respondent behave, when is it permissible for one to become a reasoner, how they can be specific yet discontinuous, where it is appropriate for objection or opposition and when must one remain silent in order one's opponent to speak and reason?"[1]

The Arabs devoted extensive writings to debates and paid as much attention to them as they did to any literary or intellectual genre or art, to the extent that they excelled in distinguishing between types of debates and identifying the differences between them and other types of dialogue, including the debates that were prominent in their intellectual lives. Shaykh Muhammad Abu Zahra describes the difference between debate and controversy, saying: "The terms 'debate', 'argument' and, sometimes, 'contestations' circulate on people's tongues. From time to time, one is inaccurately used in

---

1 Ibn Khaldun Al-Muqadimah Dar Al-Balkhi, Syria, first edition, 2004, vol. 2 p203

the place of another. The truth is that there are clear differences between each definition, for the intention behind a debate is to reach the truth about a topic in which the participants' views differ; and the purpose of an argument is to compel the opponent and overcome them by reasoning."[1]

One of the basic characteristics of dialogue in Arab culture is its connection to morality, so we often find books about the etiquette of behaviour and the ethics of dialogue, such as the book "The Ethics of Scholars" by hadith jurist Muhammad bin Hussain Abu Bakr Al-Ajeri (d.360 AH). Imam Al-Ghazali in his book "Ihya' 'Ulum Al-Din" also focused on the subject of debate, its etiquette and its impact on literature and thought, to which he devoted his entire fourth chapter. Here we also cite Ibrahim bin Muhammad Al-Bayhaqi's book "Virtues and Deficiencies", whose appearance dates back to the start of the 11th century CE and another book which some attribute to Al-Jahiz ,"Virtues and their Opposites".

Let us examine the shining examples of cultural dialogue in Islamic civilisation in the first half of the second century AH / ninth century CE through the reports of the historian Imam Al-Dhahabi: "Khalaf ibn Al-Muthanna said: 'People who were unparalleled in their divergence with reference to religion sat in a majlis in Basra, the like of which had not been witnessed before: Al-Khalil bin Ahmad Al-Farahidi, author of "Al'Uruud" and a Sunni; Al-Sayyid bin Muhammad Al-Himyari, a Shi'ite; Salih bin Abdul-Quddus, a heretic; Sufyan bin Mujashi', a Safawi Khariji; Bashshar bin Burd, a lewd libertine; Hammad 'Ajrad, a heretic; Ras Al-Jalut, who was Jewish; ibn Nazeer, the spokesperson for Christians; Amr Al Mu'ayyad, a Magian; and Ruh bin Sinan Al-Harrani, a Sabean. This group recited poems, and Bashshar used to say: 'These verses of yours, oh so-and-so are far better than such and such a surah

---

1   Abu Zahra, Tarikh al-Jadal, Dar Al-Fikr Al-Arabi, Cairo, p 5

(chapter in the Qur'an). It is due to this type of joke and others like it that Bashshar was deemed to be a blashphemer and an apostate."[1]

The spread of majilis contributed to the creation of widespread intellectual activity in the cities of Islam that affected all those working in knowledgeable fields in the Islamic West as well. Scholars also reported on the controversy and intellectual freedom that was taking place in Baghdad between people of various religions and sects, not to mention the story reported by Imam Muhammad bin Futuh Al Humaydi Al-Andalusi about Abu Muhammad Abdullah bin Abi Zayd's (from Kairouan) meeting with Abu 'Umar Ahmad bin Muhammad bin Sa'ad Al-Maliki (The Andalusian) and his questions regarding what he attended in Baghdad, and about the gatherings of scholars during the life of Abu Bakr Muhammad bin Abdullah bin Salih Al-Abhari (the Malikite), who lived between 289-375 AH / 902-986 CE). One day he asked him: "Have you attended the majilis of Ahl-al-Kalam?" He answered, "Yes, I attended them twice. Then I abandoned their gatherings and did not return to them." Abu Muhammad asked; "Why?" He answered "As for the first majlis I attended, I saw that it brought together all the sects – Muslims were in attendance who were both from Ahl al-Sunnah (mainstream Islam) and those who were innovators. Disbelievers were also in attendance – Magians, secularists, heretics, Jews, Christians and all other sects who disbelieve (in Islam). Each group had a leader who speaks for their own sect and defends it. Whenever the leader of any other group entered or approached, regardless of who they are or the group that they represent, everyone would stand up to honour him and would only sit down when he began to do so. When the majlis was replete with attendees; and there remained nobody else that was expected, one of the disbelievers would announce: "You have gathered here today for a

---

1   Shams Al-Din Al-Dhahabi, Tarikh Al-Islam, vol. 9 ed. Amr Abdussalam Al-Tadmuri, Dar Al-Kitab Al-'Arabi, Beirut, second edition, 1413 AH / 1993 CE p 383

debate, a disputation, so that the Muslims should not protest against us using their Book, nor say amongst themselves 'no, we do not believe in this, nor do we acknowledge that.' Rather, we will debate using only arguments of reason and analogy until the concur and say 'Yes, you own that (point).' " Abu 'Umar said: "when I heard that, I did not return to the gathering. Then I was told that there was another gathering that centred on theology, so I went to attend it; and found that they were held in the same manner as that of their companions, so I refrained permanently from attending the majilis of ahl al-kalam". Abu Muhammad then asked: "And were the Muslims (in the gathering) content with these happenings?" Abu 'Umar replied: "This is what I witnessed", which caused Abu Muhammad to wonder greatly."[1]

Religious discussions were widespread in councils and even in mosques. These have been translated in a number of works, including what was mentioned in the seventh century AH in the book of Sa'd bin Mansur bin Kammuna the Jew, "Revising Research on the Three Sects: Judaism, Christianity and Islam". Thus, the phenomenon of majilis became widespread in order to enrich cultural dialogue between adherents of faith in most regions of the Islamic world. Here, Ibn Hazm Al-Andalusi demonstrates the sunnah of difference, indicating the religious pluralism that existed throughout the length and breadth of Arab civilisation, emphasising the element of difference: "The lands were never free of diversity. Those who differed in the matter of schools of thought were not more than those who followed the doctrine of Malik in Andalusia and Africa; and there were whole groups of scholars who disagreed with it entirely. This is something that we witness all the time; and is nothing more than the superiority of Islam over the countries which it dominated – may Allah be praised – there

---

1 Muhammad bin Futuh Al-Hamidi Al-Andalusi, Jathwat Al-Muqtabas fi dhikr wulat Al-Andalus Al-Dar Al-Masriyyah lil ta'lif wal nashr, Cairo 1966 p 110

exist, concurrently, huge numbers of Jews, Christians, Magians and polytheists. We state this in order to underline two very necessary and conclusive pieces of evidence, or proofs. The first of which is that people's original state is the existence of diversity in their opinions based on what we presented before portraying their varying natures and purposes. The second is that Allah the Most High has decreed this himself, saying: 'Had your Lord so willed, He would have certainly made humanity one single community [of believers], but they will always [choose to] differ' (Hud: 118). So, it is right and proper that the heterogeneity is our natural state, one which we will always remain upon and one that we have been created for, except for the minority."[1]

One of the important moments that drew my attention with reference to the culture of difference and dialogue in Andalusia – that beacon of refined co-existence in the Middle Ages – is the manifestation of this in the personalities of Ibn Rush (1126 – 1198) and Ibn Maimun (1204 – 1135). The co-existence of Jews in the Arab-Islamic context greatly enabled the Jewish thinkers' creativity. Here, their intellectual production was at its most prolific and prosperous, and Ibn Maimun's book "Guide for the Perplexed", which was very clearly influenced by Ibn Rushd's philosophy, gained prominent status amongst those working in Jewish philosophy. One anecdote tells of Ibn Maimun's student, Yusuf bin 'Aqnin, who writes a letter, replete with literary metaphors, to his teacher, expressing his love for his teacher's 'daughter' – an allegory for the reconciliation of theology and philosophy – and earnest desire to marry her. "This girl pleased me, so I entered into engagement with her according to Shariah law and what was revealed on Mount Sinai; and I married her with three things: by giving her my love as a dowry, I presented her (control of) my

---

[1] Ibn Hazm Al-Andalusi, Al-Ihkam fi usul Al-Ahkam, ed Shaykh Ahmad Muhammad Shakir, vol. 4 Dar alUfuq Aljadeeda, Beirut, p 183

desire as her contract, for I am infatuated by her; and I treated her as a husband would his virgin wife. After this, I wished for her to be enthroned, seated regally, on the marital bed, for I did not take her as a temptation or foolishness, but rather she matched my love with hers and linked my soul to hers." All of this took place in the presence of two famous justices, namely Abu 'Ubayd Allah (ibn Maimun) and Ibn Rushd.[1]

This is an image of dialogue in a majlis of diverse religious and sectarian backgrounds, proving the connection that dialogue has in Islamic civilisation with the right to difference, and acceptance of and respect for others, which are all inherent components of our civilisation that impact all levels of religion, intellect and politics. This was reflected in the literature of the Umayyad and Abbasid eras in particular, during which Arab poetry classified as "Naqa'id" flourished and received much interest from members of the public – scholars, rulers and poets of the era such as Al-Farazdaq, Jarir, Al-Akhtal, Al-Ba'ith and others.

These poems are written in adversarial style, replete with boastful accounts of noble lineage and other desirable characteristics. Despite Islam's disapproval of this type of poetry, it has enriched the Arabic language and preserved many of the words and phrases that would otherwise have become extinct. In fact, these Naqa'id are also considered to be a rich, first-hand historical record of the Arabs' daily routines – events, lineages, families and tribes – both before and during Islam.

This atmosphere of dialogue indicated the Arabs' expansive horizons which attracted historians, including the American Will Durant who said: "In societies that were more literary than these, people listened to the songs of poets or to the verses of the Qur'an. Amongst them, they established philosophical seminars, such as

---

1   Ahmad Shahlan: Ibn Rushd wal fikr Al-'Arabi Alwasit, Almaktaba wal warraqa alwataniyyah, Marrakech, first edition, 1999, p 210

Ikhwan Al-Safa. Historians tell of a club that existed around the year 790 CE, consisting of these members: a Sunni, a Shi'ite, a Kharijite, a poet who writes love poetry, a materialist philosopher, a Christian, a Jew, a Sabean and a Zoroastrian. Historians report that the meetings of these members were dominated by a spirit of mutual tolerance, sweet humour and calm discussion characterised by politeness and courtesy.[1]

International Majalis and the Patronage of Senior Princes and Ministers

Books that belong to our heritage contain many gems on the richness of dialogue and its effects on intellectual and social life – this heritage attests to the reverence that many princes and ministers have for councils of dialogue. It is narrated that there was an author and powerful figure in the world of debates, Al-Huthayl (d. 227 AH / 824 CE) who was known as "Milas". He was a Magian who converted to Islam following his attendance at the majlis of the minister Yahya bin Khalid Al-Barmaki. On one occasion the minister asked a group of orators and masters about the truth of love. Amongst them was Al-Huthayl who waited for his turn and then said: "Oh minister, love seals the sights and lays an imprint on the hearts. Its pasture is the body and its origin the liver. Its owner is a disposer of suspicions and delusions. What he hopes for and what is promised are never delivered to him. Calamities rush toward him. It is a dose of the infusion of death yet has a softness that is present in nature and enhances appearance. Its owner is a horse who will not obey cautionary commands."[2] In all, there were 13 speakers, and Al-Huthayl was the third of

---

1   Willy Durant The Story of Civilisation tr. Zaki Naguib Mahmoud and others, vol. 13 Dar Al-Jll, Beirut and Lebanon, ALSESCO, Tunis 1408 AH / 1988 CE p166
2

their number to speak. Were it not for fear of length, I would have mentioned all their words put together.[1]

Another example of this rich dialogue is the debate that took place between Al-Serafy and Matta bin Yunus, the Christian, at the majlis of the Abbasid minister Ibn Al-Furat in the year 326 AH/938 CE, told to us by Abu Hayyan Al-Tawhidi in his book "Al-Mu'anasah":

"Then, oh Shaykh – may God preserve you for the people of knowledge and enliven your students by you – I mentioned a debate that took place in the majlis of the minister, Abu Al-Fath Al-Fadl bin Ja'afar ibn Al-Furat, between Abu Sa'id Al-Serafy and Abu Bishr Matta; and I summarised it. Abu Al-Fath said to me: "Transcribe this debate in full, because something is going on in that noble meeting between these two Shaykhs who are in the presence of those eminent people, the wisdom of which must be gleaned, its benefits known and none of its contents neglected." So, I wrote: "Abu Sa'id told me a summary of this story." As for 'Ali bin 'Isa Al-Shaykh Salih, he narrated it in full, with explanation: When the majlis was held in the year three hundred and twenty six, Minister Ibn Al-Furat said to the group – amongst whom were Al-Khalidi, ibn Al-Akhshad, Al-Kutbi, Ibn Abi Bishr, Ibn Rabah bin Ka'b, Abu Qudamah bin Ja'afar, Al-Zuhri, Ali bin 'Issa Al-Jarrah, Ibn Firas, Ibn Rashid, Ibn Abdul 'Aziz Al-Hashimi, Ibn Yahya Al-Alawi, Rasul bin Tughj from Egypt and Al-Mazarbani, the companion of Al-Saman: 'Will you not delegate someone from amongst you to debate with Matta using logic, for he says: "There is no way to know truth from falsehood, truth from lies, good from evil, argument from suspicion or doubt from certainty except by what we know and have internalised of logic, based on our ability to implement it and benefit from it as granted by The Creator according to the levels and limits that He has

---

[1] Shams Al-Din bin Khalkan, Wafiyat Al-A'yan wa anba' abna' alzaman, ed Ihsan Abbas, Dar Al-Sadr, Beirut, first edition, vol. 4 p 266

set'." The people hesitated and bowed. Ibn Al-Furat said: "By God, there are those amongst you who stand true to what they say; and those who debate and break (go against) what they say. Here, I stand before you and promise you a master of knowledge, a supporter of the faith and its people, and a beacon for truth and all those who seek it. So, what is this whispering and winking that you surreptitiously engage in?" Abu Sa'id Al-Serafy lifted his head and said: "Apologies, Minister, for the knowledge that lies protected in the heart is not the knowledge that is presented in this majlis to attentive ears, observant eyes, sharp minds and critical hearts. For this brings prestige, and prestige is broken. It attracts modesty; and modesty is overcome, for filth in a private battle is not to be compared with a public place." Ibn Al-Furat said: "You, Abu Sa'id, are worthy. Your apology on behalf of others requires you to have attained victory within yourself, and your victory reflects upon that of the group." Abu Sa'id said: "Disagreement with the Minister's plans is wrong, and refraining from his opinion is a certain path to destruction. We seek refuge in God from missteps and we ask Him for the best of assistance both in times of war and in times of peace." Then he confronted Matta and said: "Speak to me of logic, what do you mean by it? For if we understand what you mean by it, then our response to you would be to accept its correctness and reject its errors according to our familiar methods and accepted traditions…" (The original historical text continues until the end of the two men's conversation).[1]

Translation is the Mirror of the Islamic Civilisation and its International Capital

The predominant belief over the years has been that Arabs are nothing more than a link between the Greeks and the West, due

---

1 Abu Hayyan Al-Tawhidi, Al-Imta' wal mu'anasah, Al Maktabah Al'Asriyyah, Beirut, first edition, 1424 AH p 90

to the huge volume of translation works undertaken by Arab and Muslim intellectuals in the Abbasid era. This is a belief that does a huge injustice to the creative role played by the translation movement over the centuries.

Translation is a sublime form of dialogue between nations and is not limited to transmitting knowledge and literature. Rather, it is based on offering service and harnessing benefit, on influencing and being influenced, for the Arab Islamic culture has, undoubtedly, been influenced by the Greek legacy after its translations, just as it was influenced by the legacies of ancient India and ancient China. Receiving this legacy was by of thorough, careful consideration of it, by diligence and enrichment.

Throughout various important eras, the translation movement expressed a civilisational need for nations to develop their knowledge, organise their communication and expand their networks. This movement occupied individuals' thought as much as it occupied the concerns of groups and countries, in fact, since ancient times it has taken on both scientific and cognitive dimensions, as it far exceeded the boundaries of linguistic communication and went on to form a mill of cognitive dialogue.

We acknowledge that all nations and civilisations have benefited from translation to the point that it shapes their destiny, for there is no civilisation that has not learnt from the other. Civilisations, in their turn, both influence and are influenced by others through the process of translation. Therefore, everything that lies at the service of humanity today in terms of technological progress, prosperity and intellectual development are the fruits of this process of mutual influence, and the vehicle is translation. Nobody can claim that the progress they achieve is fashioned by them alone, for traces of the ancients and previous nations are to be found in every contribution we make towards progress, because whatever progress has been collectively earned was made by the whole of humanity. Translation, through the ages, has always been a bridge of communication between peoples and civilisations – facilitating meeting and acquaintance, opening windows through which they may gaze out at the multiplexity of cultures, and encouraging people towards creativity by showcasing what other nations have achieved in the past.

Translation has gifted us the opportunity to view history from a different perspective than any division of eras according to the history of empires and states. We can definitely state that the brightest moments in the history of humanity were those associated with the availability of translation, its spread and its adoption as an essential tool in presenting the results of progress or bringing about rapprochement between peoples so that they could contribute to the improvement of human life. The Greeks experienced the pinnacle of their civilisation when they translated the treasures of science and art from other ancient civilisations such as the Persian and the Egyptian. Likewise, the Arab-Islamic civilisation's most wonderful moments came when its translations were transformed into one of the Abbasid state's greatest investments; we have the best and most powerful example of this in the establishment of Bayt Al Hikmah (The House of Knowledge), Al-Ma'mun's legacy which was adopted as a means towards civilisational progress.

The House of Wisdom was a prominent project of the Abbasid Empire. When remembering the Abbasid era, we cannot neglect this incredible intellectual project that not only spread throughout the Islamic world, but whose fruits are still being used by humanity to this very day. One of translation's characteristics is that it preserves the scientific and intellectual heritage of civilisations by transferring it to other languages, so that it continues to live on again and again. It is important to point out that the translation movement from Greek to Arabic was not limited to the patronage of Muslim caliphs, but it was a grassroots social and intellectual movement in which the educated classes and anyone who was a keen seeker of knowledge was interested, because the tradition of dialogue, deeply rooted in Arab Islamic society was not only the concern of the "cultured elite", but permeated deeply throughout society as a whole.

Here we recall what Ibn Abi 'Usayba'ah narrated of Al-Ma'mun in his book "'Uyun al-anba' fi tabaqat al-atiba'": "When Al-Ma'mun saw his informed vision, it was as if he saw a shaykh with beautiful appearance, sitting on a pulpit whilst he was giving a sermon, saying 'I am Aristotle'. He woke from his slumber; and asked who Aristotle was. He was informed that he was a wise man from Greece, so he summoned Hunayn bin Ishaq to him. He found none to be his equal in transcription, so he asked him to transcribe the books of Greek scholars into the Arabic language, bestowing money and gifts upon him. So this vision was one of the strongest reasons behind the books, for there was substantial correspondence between Al-Ma'mun and the Persian emperor, and Al-Ma'mun had already written to the emperor seeking permission to choose whatever he wanted from the ancient sciences stored at his disposal. After a period of thought, the emperor responded positively. So, Al-Ma'mun selected a group, who included Al-Hajaj bin Matar and Ibn Al-Batriq, and they chose items for him. When these were brought to him, Al-Ma'mun ordered them to copy them, which they did. It was said that Yuhanna bin Masawayh was amongst those who were sent to translate these books, and that Al-Ma'mun also included Hunayn bin Ishaq who was young at the time. He ordered Hunayn to translate as much as he could from the books of the Greek sages and to correct what others had written, so Hunayn complied. It was also said that Al-Ma'mun used to give him the weight of each book he translated to Arabic in gold, like for like. [1]

There is no doubt whatsoever that Al-Ma'mun expanded the circle of interest in the House of Wisdom, redoubled its activity,

---

1   Ibn Abi 'Usaybiyyah Al-Khazraji, 'Uyun Al-anba' fi taabaqat al-atibba', ed. Nazar Rida, Dar Maktabat Al-Hayat, Beirut, p261

attracted translators and urged them to transfer knowledge by sending them to Constantinople to bring back whatever important Greek works they could.

Dimitri Gutas, professor of Arabic literature at Yale University, confirms this message with great fairness of approach: "We make it clear, above all, that the Greek-Arabic translation movement extended over the span of more than two centuries and was not an ephemeral phenomenon. Secondly, it was supported by the entire elite of Abbasid society – caliphs, princes, state employees, military leaders, merchants, bankers and scholars – it was not a project that was limited to a specific group or sector. Thirdly, support was provided by allocating huge public subsidies and massive private contributions – it was neither an abnormal whim nor an act of social bravado carried out by wealthy individuals who aspired to donate to a humanitarian cause or for self-aggrandisement."[1]

Objective historians of science comment that the stage of Arabic translation is undoubtedly one of the most important glories of the Arab-Islamic civilisation, clear-cut evidence of its openness and interaction with other civilisations. However, many neglect a bright moment in the history of the translation movement – Andalusia. Muslims in Andalusia were interested in translating Arabic books and other works into the Latin and Castillian languages, and Andalusia became known as the centre of translation and the Arabisation movement, which reached its peak during the 10th century CE with the participation of the bishops who established translation institutes in the city of Toledo. Here, dozens of traditional Arabic heritage works in various disciplines such as philosophy, astronomy and medicine were translated. It is important to note here that translation in Andalusia was an integral part of the life of intellectuals, intertwined with reading and writing.

---

1   Dimitri Gutas, Greek Thought and Arab Culture, tr. and presented by Nichola Ziyadeh, The Arab Organisation for Translation, first edition 2003 p 31

There is no doubt that Europe was revived in the 15th century, the time of its renaissance, thanks to the translation of Andalusian heritage that came from the Islamic West. For decades I have believed that interaction between nations requires resources, and this is not possible without translation because translation is the essential tool for acculturation. In all aspects of my life, I have recognised the importance of this method, to the extent that when I took over the Ministry of Culture, Arts and Heritage in Qatar, I took the initiative to establish a translation project, and it became a crucible of successful experiments in cultural communication between peoples, their cultures and literatures. I was certain that all civilizations and nations benefited from translation, in fact it became an integral part of their destiny. There is absolutely no civilisation that has not learned from others. Throughout their natural cycle civilizations both influence and are affected by others through the process of translation. Therefore, everything that is available to humanity today in terms of progress, technical prosperity and intellectual development, is the fruit of this process of mutual influence – and the vehicle is translation. Nobody can claim that the progress they achieve is fashioned by them alone, for traces of the ancients and previous nations are to be found in every contribution we make towards progress, because that progress has been collectively earned by the whole of humanity. Translation, through the ages, has always been a bridge of communication between peoples and civilisations – facilitating meeting and acquaintance, opening windows through which they may gaze out at the multiplexity of cultures; and encouraging people towards creativity by showcasing what other nations have achieved in the past.

Followers of monotheistic faiths throughout Islamic history freely enjoyed reading and writing. In fact, Ibn Abi Usaiba'h mentions a brief biography of Muwaffaq Al-Din ibn Al-Mutran, who had a great desire to collect books. He died, leaving medical treaties and other books, approximately 10,000 foreign volumes.

He took meticulous and excessive care in copying, transcribing and editing books and he had three scribes, or copyists in his service who were constantly writing for him. Amongst them was Jamal Al-Din, known also as Ibn Al-Jamalah – to whom his handwriting was attributed. Ibn Al-Mutran also wrote many books in his own hand and I have seen several of them that were the very epitome of perfect handwriting, correctness and syntax. He was a voracious reader of books and would read for the majority of his time. Most of the books that were in his possession had been corrected and edited by him; his handwriting was visible throughout. He was so passionately devoted to books and the search for knowledge that he collected many small booklets and scattered treaties and articles on medicine, then gathered them all into one single volume. He also copied small portions for himself and his own personal perusal. He cut off a one-sixteenth piece of Al-Baghdadi's writings with a ruler, copying them in his own handwriting. He would always glean as much as he could and would constantly have a volume tucked up his sleeve so that he could read it at the door of the sultan's house, or whenever he had a free moment wherever he went. All his books were sold after his death, because he did not leave behind a son.[1] Ibn Abi Usaiba'h also mentioned what Al-Hakimm Imran Al-Isra'ili told him about the circumstances of selling Ibn Al-Mutran's books, having found many precious finds and pearls of wisdom in them, including books in Ibn Al-Jamalah's handwriting.

And say: "Go forth unto the world."

Since dialogue is a journey towards the other, how many Arab travellers have given wonderful examples in their journeys of their communication with other peoples and cultures? They commissioned calligraphers to describe their movements just as

---

1   See: Ibn Abi Usaybi'ah 'Uyun Al-Anba' Op. cit. tr. Muwaffaq Al-Din ibn Al-Matran

the Sultan ordered the documentation of Ibn Battuta's travels. These trips were not for any particular religious purpose, as much as they were for discovery, cooperation and knowledge exchange. The itineraries of these trips clearly reflected recognition of the other. These trips were rich mines of documentation that recorded human, architectural and geographical features of the world and contributed to expanding the horizons of dialogue and participation. Despite the differences between travellers in the way in which they recorded their experiences, they nevertheless documented all that they saw and heard, providing us with a substantial and precious body of knowledge that has benefited and continues to benefit sociologists, economists and historians of literature and religions. This is not to mention that Arab travellers during the Middle Ages demonstrated skills superior to those of geographers. These travellers preserved the geographical material created by Greek scholars such as Ptolemy and Pliny, in addition to observing, monitoring and documenting geographical phenomena whilst describing countries, cities and populations along with their demographic distributions throughout the region. Most trips contained a phenomenal amount of knowledge in the fields of geography, history and sociology. They also did not neglect the human aspect of their voyages. The traveller was, anthropologically, an active participant in events, not merely a detached observer of them. The traveller met people, learned about their lifestyles and shared their livelihoods for significant periods of time.

Who amongst us, whether in Arab or western scientific circles does not know of Ibn Battuta - one of the most renowned of Arab voyagers, famous for his travels that lasted almost 30 years, during which he visited all the countries of the known world at the time. And who amongst us has not read at least a small part of his inspirational book, "Tuhfat an-nuzzar fi ghara'ib al-amsar wa 'aja'ib asfar" which has been translated into more than 50 different languages, in which he documents his observations of the social and economic phenomena in the Arabian Gulf region, which he visited twice, and got to know most of its cities and ports – Dhofar, the Arabian Sea and Oman. Ibn Battuta describes places and foods, he outlines doctrines, traditions, languages and dialects, and he describes the most significant economic activities including, of course, those specific to pearl diving. Ibn Battuta pays the most meticulous detail in his report and is precise in his observations. Speaking about the people of Dhofar, he said: "Among their good traditions is shaking hands in the mosque after the morning and afternoon prayers. The people in the first line leaned towards the qiblah. Those who come in behind them are also in line and shake hands with them. They do the same after the Friday prayer, where they all shake hands with one another. One of the wonderous things about this city is that no-one intends harm to it except that a misfortune befalls him or something comes between him and it." [1]

Ibn Battuta does not let a meaningful anecdote go by without mentioning it or documenting it in his writing. This is pleasurable for the reader and demonstrates the value of his observations as well as his intimate knowledge of the culture of the peoples amongst whom he is a guest. He tells his stories succinctly with a great deal of wisdom: "It is narrated that the king Kabak spoke to the jurist and preacher Badr Al-Din Al-Maidani one day, asking: "You say that God has mentioned everything in His Mighty Book?" He replied: "Yes" So he asked: "Where is my name, then?" Badr Al-Din answered: "In the words of Allah the Exalted:

فِى أَىِّ صُورَةٍ مَّا شَآءَ رَكَّبَكَ Fi ayyi suratin ma sha'a rakabak – Into whatsoever form He will, He casteth thee (Al-Infitar : 8)." This pleased him, so he replied "yakhsha", meaning 'good' in Turkish. He honoured him greatly and continued to glorify Muslims. [2]

---

1 Muhammad bin Abdullah bin Muhammad Al-lawati Al-tunji, Ibn Battuta Tuhfat al nathar fi ghara'ib al-amsar wa aja'ib al-asfar, Hindawi Foundation 2017 p184
2 Op. cit. p 262

Whatever the degree of honesty in transmitting, describing and appreciating cultural diversity from one traveller to another, Arab explorers' travel journals and travel literature contributed significantly to demonstrating their efforts and sincere intentions during their voyages of discovery and understanding the 'Other'. Al-Baghdadi Ahmad bin Fadlan's journey into the unknown heart of northern Europe revealed his merit and skills in describing the heritage and culture of the inhabitants of these regions to his readers, as their history was almost entirely unknown and completely absent from any written sources. His journey took 11 months, during which he took great care to describe, or comment on, everything he saw. He mentioned the smallest of details which later contributed to helping the descendants of these regions understand their own ancestors' lifestyles. When he visited the Russian regions, he gave a very precise description of their people: "I saw the Russians who had come to trade and they descended on the Atl river. Their bodies and posture were tall, lithe palm trees, their hair blonde or flaming red. They wore neither earrings nor slippers, but each man wore a long garment that entirely encased half of their body vertically with an arm hole through which his hand appeared. Each man carried an axe, a sword and a knife which they kept on their persons at all times."[1]

Let us look, too, at the journey of Shihab Al-Din Ahmad bin Qasim Al-Hajri – also known as Afwaqi. He describes a debate with Jews in Frankish lands, Holland to be precise, during his trip there between 1611 and 1613. After having read the Torah in Andalusian, and after having met with various Frankish scholars who lavished praise on their religion, he answered them from their eloquent books: "Amongst the issues that the Jews spoke to me of

---

[1] Ibn Fadlan, Risalat ibn Fadlan fi wasf alrihla ila bilad al-turk wal khazar wal rus wal saqalibah, ed. Sami Al-Dahhan, AlMujama' Alilmi printing press, Damascus & Al Matba' al Hashimi, 1960 p 149

was that our ancient origin is descended from our Prophet Ismail, peace be upon him, and that his mother is not like the mother of Prophet Ishaq, peace be upon him, because she was the wife of our master Abraham, a freewoman, whilst the mother of Ismail, peace be upon him, was owned. I told them everything that the prophets, peace be upon them, did was in direct accordance with what God almighty has permitted. They then asked me a question that they think nobody can answer." They said: "The religion upon which our master, Moses, peace be upon him, was upon was from God." I replied "Yes, there is no dispute between us on this matter." They responded: "The sultans of this world use the books as a guide." I answered: "They use nothing as a source except that which befits them and in certain ages only. In our belief, God The Almighty erases what He wills and confirms what He wills." They enquired: "Where is this to be found in the Torah?", we replied: "In chapter 20 of the second book of sultans."[1]

Thus, these travel journals constituted a reliable source for the study of history, archaeology, sociology and anthropology. They presented the travellers' realistic impressions and personal observations. Just as it benefitted historians and geographers, it also became highly prized travel literature, a subtle genre that combines the characteristics of story-telling, narrative and autobiography which confirms the Arabs' skill in transforming their journeys in real-life into an art that is replete with observations and showcases different nations' lifestyles, cultures, social relations and worldview. The journeys of Arab explorers reflect the constant dialogue with other nations and express Arab openness and willingness to discover worlds beyond their own, in addition to their search for knowledge wherever it may be found. By doing so, Arab culture

---

1   Ahmad bin Qassim Alhajeri, Rihlat Afwaqi Al-Andalusi, ed and presented by Muhammad Razzouq, Swedish publishing house, Arab Foundation for research and publication, 1st edition, 2004 p 89

was enriched by any number of intellectual, historical and urban treasures. Furthermore, they became familiar with the principal traits of the other nations and their lifestyles, which enabled them to broaden their own horizons and enhance their perspective towards an expansive and welcoming civilisation, not one that is closed and hostile.

Conclusion
Mutual Understanding is an Arab Mission

In my estimation, the dialogue of cultures does not stem from a need alone. Rather it is a core concept on which civilizations are founded. This concept is built on the unique Qur'anic principle of "ta'aruf" (mutual introduction and acquaintance); for when you begin a dialogue, you have embarked on the adventure of ta'aruf. By doing so, you reach out to the other and begin to build bridges, not merely pleasantries or inconsequential talk.

In any case: "Dialogue reinforces the strategy of equality and finds its justification when human existence and rights are placed at the centre of this equation. Therefore, it is necessary to define the rules of dialogue and establish them on equitable legal frameworks imbued with moral values."[1]

Mutual Understanding Means Accepting the Other

Intercultural dialogue facilitates mutual understanding between humans. It provides the ability for nations to transmit cultures between themselves through the means they have available at their

---

1 Damako, Rights and Religion in the Middle Intersection tr. Al-Majdi Muhammad, Dar Atlas, first edition, 2019, p 124

disposal and to introduce the civilization of each nation, learn of cultural nuances and glean knowledge that is compatible with their own principles and beliefs. Communication opens the door for a person to interact with other human cultures, highlighting their vital aspects and in essence going far beyond linguistic knowledge. Language is only the tip of the submerged iceberg. Often, we incorrectly believe that our inability to master another language prevents us from communication and mutual understanding. However, mastery of a foreign language does not alone guarantee mutual understanding, because one must master knowledge of the culture as well. That is why communication requires some level of intellect which we may term "the differences we hold in common". This will not be achieved if it becomes the responsibility of only one party. It is the sum of phenomena resulting from continuous and direct interaction between a group of individuals belonging to different cultures that leads to changes in the cultural patterns of the group or multiple human groups.

I have been an optimist throughout my life and, in truth, I do not know where this optimism comes from. As soon as difficult periods befell me, whilst waiting for deliverance I would often say to myself: "Intensify, oh calamity, in order but you may be speedily alleviated." My mission at UNESCO was not an exception to this rule, nor did it deviate from this principle, for after the injustices that had befallen it, whether from those closest to me or from strangers, I found myself opening doors to fresh opportunities to striving and giving. I took a few months to catch my breath, then found myself being summoned by my country's leadership to head Qatar National Library. Here, once again, I feel the precious trust that my leadership places in me, and keenly feel the patriotic responsibility that relies on the supervision of this bastion of science, culture and knowledge, which is almost unique in the Arab world, given the advanced technology that has built its formidable infrastructure, as well as the rare manuscripts that the library holds.

My responsibilities did not prevent me from thinking deeply, especially since the COVID pandemic kept us confined to our homes. I was sitting facing the sea at my home in Ras Laffan in northern Qatar and I was beset by many questions: where is humanity heading? Is it hurtling towards annihilation and death by weapons of mass destruction, or will it board a ship and arrive on safe shores, or remain part of the convoy that journeys across the desert in solidarity? How is it possible for humanity's ship to survive the floods and avoid sinking in this ocean of choppy waters? I used to believe, and still do, that the main element at stake here is one of culture, despite the constant fluctuations of politics and vested interests that govern it. To me, it expresses both ethical and social responsibility in internal, external, national and international policies.

I believe in humanity's quest to achieve progress and prosperity for all human beings. Everyone on earth deserves to live under equitable values – regardless of their location, ideology religion or gender. For this land is for everyone and these values belong to everybody, and all nations have nurtured it with their cultures and languages over the ages.

I also believe in the contributions of Arabic culture and its role in achieving the goals that humanity has outlined, as long as they remain loyal to the principles of tolerance, love, coexistence, harmony and human rights. Just as they seek to remain protected by these principles, they also preserve their own unique features, remaining true to themselves and open to others, relying on dialogue and respect of those around them.

Global modernity sought to bridge the gaps between local culture and global culture, between global culture and popular culture, and between the elite and the masses. Therefore, we look forward to going beyond what has already been achieved, striving for the better and exceeding what we already have by striving harder and harnessing the will and determination of those who believe in the eternal future of morals and generations. This determination and will stems from freedom and for me it is based entirely on reason, not on whims and desires, simply because it is based on the moral duty to be ethical. Thus, a person would start to sculpt their own being from the essence of their human dignity, then the entity of their nation, and from there participate in creating human civilization. Therefore, despite their patriotism and pride in homeland and culture, the individual remains a global citizen. They feel happy when people are joyful and saddened by their misery. They strive to disseminate values of peace using all the means at their disposal, including literature and arts that refer to common values in a fascinating ascetic dimension. The hope of changing minds still continues as long as the will to do so exists, as long as our faith in what we share in common is unshakable. As long as we believe in what brings us together, we are capable of actualising our humanity and our universality despite our differences, because our destiny remains one and the same and because this earth belongs to us all.

This necessitates a common global understanding around the protection of the environment because it has a direct impact on the future of humanity, as is spreading awareness and knowledge to the most vulnerable and fragile communities that are more exposed to natural disasters such as those in Africa, Asia, Latin America and the smaller developing islands.

Confronting these challenges requires the wise to become active and empowered in the use of all available means in order to develop scientific research that will help address these repercussions, such as the dangers of technological progress and dramatic climate change. This does not negate the need to draw up proactive policies to reduce these risks, policies that are built on international mutual understandings and policies that do not neglect to link our concern for environmental health with food security and cultural roots. Here, we confirm UNESCO's central role in the same way that the statement from the 2015 United Nations Climate Change Conference in Paris and other subsequent statements were historic landmarks that contributed to combating the phenomenon of global warming that threatens the planet. What causes us to view the planet of humans with some modicum of optimism is the emergence of a kind of cross-cultural citizenship embodying the deep faith in the unity of the human race, both now and in the future. When direct communication has been made easy between humans of different religions, races, colours and genders, they knew there was no place for them on this common plane we call Earth except through the mediums of communication and dialogue. This is where a culture of humility, respect and mutual cooperation begins.

A Glut in the North and Famine in the South

The murder of George Floyd on the 25th May 2020 under the knee of white police officer Derek Chauvin, triggered a tsunami of denunciation and indignation from Minneapolis in the United States of America to all parts of the world. Millions of people watched this heinous crime thanks to the video that was recorded and published by a teenage girl who happened to be near the scene of the murder. This daring girl was awarded the Pulitzer Special Press Prize for her courage and the courts in which the perpetrator was tried used this video as part of the prosecutor's evidence that helped to indict him. Paradoxes are many in our globalised time, swinging from the spirits of global citizenship on the one hand to racial discrimination on the other. We notice another paradox between the nations of the North and the South which many call the digital gap, or digital poverty. Fortunately, free and wise men and women of the world denounce all kinds of disparity between nations. For example, the majority of Nobel literature prize winners are almost unanimous in their agreement regarding the North's exploitation of the South. The Nigerian author Wole Soyinka reminds us of colonialist exploitation, persecution and ethnic arrogance when he speaks openly about countries that haemorrhage huge amounts of resources purchasing arms instead of building schools, libraries and hospitals. This is what I said to the face of the United States' ambassador to UNESCO when I submitted my nomination, reminding him that the cost of one single American air missile would be enough to settle America's debt to UNESCO.

In the same way, the author Le Clézio states that combating illiteracy and combating famine are intimately intertwined. He is of the opinion that an author cannot address the hungry about either food or knowledge. Doris Lessing who won the Nobel literature prize in 2007 did not ignore the glut of the North with reference to access to knowledge or the South's need of it. She tells us that she realised people's thirst for books despite their harsh economic conditions during her visit to Zimbabwe. They would beg her, saying: "We beseech you - send us books when you return to London!" On the other hand, one of the masters in a prestigious private school in north London told her: "As you know, many of our students never read. Half of the available books in the library are never used!" This is a gruesome picture of the glut of the North; and famine will be imminent in our day, as we witness libraries in the United States throwing books away due to their abundance and the lack of library storage space. When will humans take heed; and when will they realise that their excess of food or surplus books could just be what others are sorely in need?

Taking into consideration everything that has taken place and all of the above, I remain confident that goodness is anchored in humanity; for our noble Prophet - peace be upon him - has taught us that "Creation are all the children of God; and the most beloved of His creation to Him are those who are most beneficial to their children".[1] Similarly, it is narrated that Hassan Al-Basri, may God

---

1   Narrated by Anas bin Malik, ra, narrated by Al Bazar and Al-Tabarani in their collections.

have mercy on him, used to forbid hypocrisy and artificiality, saying: "Oh son of Adam – do not perform any goodness out of arrogance and do not desist from performing it out of modesty."